THE PSYCHIC CODE

Bríd O'Donoghue

ISBN 978-1-7393163-2-7

This book is dedicated to my cousin, Thomas Sharry. His final days were spent on the battle fields of Belgium, far from his native rocky shores of Newquay, in the Burren, on the West Coast of Ireland. He died as he had lived, following his belief that he should do the right thing for his fellow man.

Ar Dheis Dé go raibh sé.

(May his soul be at peace).

ACKNOWLEDGEMENTS

Many have helped with this creation, from words of encouragement to words of wisdom, I am grateful to you all, with special thanks to Bernie for your help and support.

My sincere gratitude to those who took the time to write and share their very personal stories and testimonials. These form an integral part of this book and help bring clarity and reality to this important topic.

Also, a word of thanks to Naimh Faherty for cover design.

CONTENTS

INTRODUCTION

Those of us who are sensitive go through life aware of the suffering of others. But for many with this disposition it is more than an awareness. We can find ourselves immersed in the feelings of others. Empathically we can take on a copy of the emotional turmoil of another without any understanding that what we are feeling is in fact a copy of someone else's pain.

This book will introduce you to the simple daily steps that can be used to discern whether the emotions you are currently feeling are yours, or if you have picked up on the joy or turmoil of another person. It is possible to connect and disconnect from these emotions without draining your own energy in the process.

Being this sensitive to the pain of others has affected all aspects of my life: my health and wellbeing, my relationships and my decision making. Looking back at my journey from childhood, I am shocked to see how many of my actions were dictated by the energy of others. I now know that, on many occasions, had I been solid in my own energy - I would have made different choices.

Now with a new understanding of what is mine and what is not, I want to share this knowledge. It is my hope that this information will help others to come to a better understanding of themselves.

I believe many of us go through similar struggles and situations. In my endeavours to bring clarity I have given examples from my own life. Some of my clients have also graciously sent me their stories to include. This allows the reader to come to a better understanding of how their sensitivity can impact their life both positively and negatively. As some of the stories and examples are of a very personal nature I have, on occasion, changed names and some individual details to protect identity.

Occasionally I mention some of my spiritual beliefs. This is in no way intended to influence the reader, it is simply given as an example. It is for each of us to come to our own understanding and relationship with our concept of a higher power.

UNDERSTANDING SENSITIVITY

Life can be very difficult for those who are highly sensitive. Most will live life completely open to the pain of others, to the point where they themselves feel that pain. They live a life without any emotional filters or protection when in the company of others.

It is important to define the word sensitive. Some people can be insulted when they are describes in this way. The word is often used as a derogatory term, implying the person is weak. Sensitive, in its truest form, is:

'Someone who is aware of other people's needs, problems, feelings or pain and shows compassion for what the other person is going through.'

If we now look at the definition of the word empath, we will see that they are very similar. An empath is described as:

'A person who has an unusually strong ability to feel the mental and/or emotional state of another individual'.

When I use the word empathic or empathy, it is in this context rather than the more commonly used meaning of someone who shows compassion to others.

Some definitions go as far as to describe empathy and sensitivity as psychic abilities. The word psychic might scare some of us and we can be slow to own it. Whether we decide to describe ourselves as sensitive, empathic, or psychic, it is essential to know we are open to feeling the pain of others.

Unfortunately, sensitive/empathic/psychic gifts are seen by many as a negative. In my work I aim to help other empaths:

- feel empowered,
- have a greater understanding of their gift,
- know they can use their ability for the greater good,
- learn how to disconnect,
- remain safely protected,
- accept this ability as a positive instead of a negative aspect of their life,
- decipher their personal psychic code.

Everything is made from energy. People talk about feeling a vibe. This can be when we observe someone who is, for example, in distress, angry, or having a tantrum. For the majority of people, that vibration passes through their energy field unnoticed. With the empath it is a very different experience. As it passes through our energy field, we feel it as if it is our own emotion. We take on a copy of the emotion and we hold onto that copy. We can behave as if it is our own emotion and our own personal situation. I explain it as being similar to putting on an old sweater belonging to someone else, a sweater that is not of our choosing and not to our taste.

In addition to taking on copies of other people's emotions, we can also take on the physical pain, mannerisms and even the posture of another. It is important to realise that we are not taking the emotion or pain away from the other person. What we are doing is taking on a copy of how they are feeling. If they are feeling the victim of injustice, we feel that injustice. If they are depressed, then we also can feel depressed. They still have their own feelings but now there are two people feeling down and depressed.

Similarly, if we meet someone in grief, we can put a copy of their grief on top of our own feelings. If we were sad to begin with, now wearing a copy of their grief, we feel completely overwhelmed. We need to realise that the person we are picking up on is still feeling their own emotions, be that depression, injustice, grief, or sadness. By wearing their 'sweater', we are not lessening their pain in any way.

Often empaths struggle at events as there is more energy available to take on. At funerals, we can take on a copy of the loss and grief of the family. Likewise visiting someone in hospital can be very challenging. We can take on a copy of the pain, fear, distress and shock of all those that we meet in the building.

Recently I had to go to a meeting. As I got out of the car and gathered my notes, I started dropping things, I couldn't find my pen, and I was getting really flustered. On meeting the manager, I noticed how he was dropping things and was totally flustered and not at all grounded. He explained that he had just received some distressing personal news. I realised it was his energy I had stepped into while in the car park.

On another occasion I was asked to do an energy clearance at a client's home. Before setting off I tried to set the navigation system in my car, but I couldn't get it to work. I was getting angrier and angrier, until I got to the point where I wanted to throw it through the windscreen. Thankfully, I realised this was not my energy. On arriving at the client's house, she introduced me to her husband. He was one of the angriest people I have ever met. I had taken on a copy of his anger.

If I am in the company of someone who has had a stroke my speech can change. When I am with someone who has dementia, I struggle to hold my thoughts.

When we slip into a copy of someone else's energy, at some level we are aware that something is not right. We may find ourselves saying things such as;

"I'm not myself today."

"It's not like me."

"I'm all over the place."

When we feel like this, we are likely not to be in our own energy.

Ideally, we try to avoid people who are disrespectful, abusive, aggressive or manipulative. But what if it's someone just having a bad day, or down on their luck, who is sad or grieving, or depressed, lonely or anxious?

If we decide to avoid everyone who is in a negative emotional space how will we: get to work, spend time with others, go to the store, socialise, or perform our everyday tasks, since anywhere there are people, there are emotions.

What if the person we are picking up on is someone we love? Are we going to avoid them until they are feeling better? No, we can't avoid everyone who is experiencing a negative emotion.

The following is a testimonial from Lisa, an American client. She describes an appointment she had with me in March 2020. Lisa gives details on the issues raised and how learning that she is an empath has helped her understand her behaviours and release many of the burdens she carried with her in life.

MY SESSION WITH BRÍD O'DONOGHUE
March 4, 2020
LISA CASPERSON

Bríd knew nothing about me when I arrived with my friend at her home. My friend had told me about her experience with Bríd, and I craved a chance to meet with her. Bríd said, *"Weren't you lucky I had a cancellation!"* I told her how I had written my intention and repeated it to myself often for the past few days: *"I am so happy and grateful that Bríd, now has time to meet with me!!!"* She said, *"Oh, you are able to manifest."* Thankfully, this time I did!

Sitting on the couch in her treatment room, she explained she is a physical, emotional and spiritual healer and that she feels people's illnesses in her own body. She quickly pointed to a few places where she felt a bit of discomfort: lower back, knee, hip and shoulder, all areas where I have pain due to osteopenia or arthritis.

She told me that I am an empath, and that the wad of pain I carry around in my chest (she made a fist and held it exactly where I do continually sense what I, too, have described as a wad of pain) is other people's pain that I have taken on. She told me because I can feel their pain, although I wish to alleviate it, I am actually taking on a copy and thus burdening myself without helping them. Bríd explained that being an empath is a gift, but we often don't know what to do with it or how to protect ourselves.

I believe she said it doesn't even have to be someone I know. I might just be conscious that someone looks sad (I do notice people's energies all the time, or I read their eyes). It could be a shop keeper, or someone on the street I just smile at and say hello to. It makes sense to me because at times my mood can change in an instant and I will think to myself, *"What on earth?! Where did this come from?"*

She asked me my father's first name. *"Philip"* I said. She told me his spirit was with me. She asked how others in the family felt about him. I told her that although I wasn't aware of it till midlife, it seemed I was the only one who liked him. I always knew my dad loved me; I was pretty sure my mom didn't like me much. Bríd said, *"Maybe your mom thought you were on your dad's side."* Since I had recently discovered a birthday card I had made for my dad when I was quite young, and what it said, I believe that could be correct.

She asked if I would like to talk to my dad. As I recall, I told him I did know he loved me, although I felt abandoned later in life. I asked forgiveness for things I had done to hurt him, and although I believe I had already forgiven him, I told him so. I said that I realize alcohol imprisoned both my dad and my mom, and they were unable to nurture and raise us, their six children, as we needed. It was painful, but I told him that he should be proud of the

16

way each of us has sought to heal and to raise our children differently.

Then Bríd asked me if I would like to sit or lay down for healing prayers. I laid down on her treatment table.

She accurately described me as a child looking back and forth, back and forth, back and forth, like I was watching a tennis match (she showed me this with her head doing just that), while feeling the pain of everyone in my family. I wanted to be able to calm it all down – but without success.

Bríd was standing next to the table. She prayed that my dad be bathed in light, asked him to forgive me if I hurt him, and told him again that I had forgiven him. I thought to myself, I guess I was the right person to be with him when he died. I am grateful for that. Then I asked my mom to forgive me, and Bríd prayed for her.

I mentioned I wanted to forgive my grandfather for touching me inappropriately. She asked about my mom, I told her she was pretty much a vacant vessel. When in mid-life I told her about the experience, she hatefully spewed that he was probably drunk and I just wanted to blame someone else for my problems. *"She was broken,"* Bríd said, *"as was your father."* Each of us prayed for her again and for my grandfather.

Then she asked me to picture a wheelbarrow full of sweaters – she described them, grey, dirty, streaked and stained, etc. They were all the pain and negative feelings I had taken on and had been 'wearing' from other people. She dumped them out the window. She explained that when I am feeling ill at ease, down for no reason, or have that wad of discomfort in my chest, I need to picture myself taking off a sweater, naming it, and then ask God to place the person to whom it belongs in a stream of Divine light and healing. I give the duplicate to God and envision myself in God's light as well. If I am not sure if it's mine or someone else's, by doing this either way, she said, whether it belongs to you or someone else, you are both winners.

She asked me to say five things I like about myself. I got two and then struggled. I said my creativity and I don't remember the other one (perhaps my love for my children?). She carried on for me, and I remember these: honest, loyal, humorous, quirky, hard-working. I think those are true.

She asked me, *"Do you have a son you are walking on eggshells around?"* I told her about

Erik. I had just recently asked him if we could talk about our twenty-two-year estrangement. I am afraid I will say or do the wrong thing and he will disappear again. It's the elephant in the room. She prayed for light around us both and said it will be better.

Bríd asked me to picture my child-self at my door and invite her in. I saw that she was too scared to even come to the door, but I encouraged her and once she came in, Bríd asked me, *"What is she doing?"* I said, *"She's twirling around and around, wearing a dress."* Bríd said, *"I saw her twirling in a white dress in a hallway in bare feet."* I didn't tell her that our front door actually comes into a hallway; that is where I pictured her as well, barefoot and wearing a white dress. I told Bríd that I was feeling afraid, having trouble promising the little girl I could keep her safe because if evil came to the door, I would be overpowered and it could just push its way in. Bríd suggested to pray that my house be protected.

So, in the end, Bríd said, *"Will the real Lisa please stand up,"* It was a blessed time and I learned a lot and felt the power of her healing prayers.

March 12, 2020

I had my first chance to put some of my new knowledge into practice on my flight home from Ireland to New York. My initial flight had been delayed so I missed my follow-up flight to North Carolina. While sitting on the plane a paralysing fear overcame me. *"What would happen to me?!"* This fear was familiar. I realized it was the fear of my child-self – a fear of being alone and lost and unable to find my way. I soothingly spoke to my child-self and reminded her that I am now an adult and have the ability to figure it out once we arrived in New York. Even as an adult, I might be nervous, but I would take one step at a time and get myself home.

It worked! When we arrived a bit past midnight, I was offered a free hotel room, but decided not to take that. I found my way to the check-in counter of my airline, planted myself on the floor with my back against a wall, and dozed. When I woke up, there was already a short line at the counter. It was three a.m. I got standby tickets for the next two laps of my journey and made it home before noon that day. I believe the work Bríd did with me and my inner child helped me to recognise that child's fear and calm myself. Being calm, I could then make intelligent decisions.

I thank God for the gift of my meeting with Bríd, and for my friend who invited me to experience County Clare, Ireland, a very mystical and spiritual place, full of lovely people and their stories.

COLLATERAL DAMAGE

It is frequently brought to my awareness that someone I know, or have come into contact with, is in emotional turmoil. I am aware of this without being told verbally. I am aware through the changes I personally feel. By observing these unexpected changes, I am more aware of the struggles of others. Once it has come to my awareness that someone is sad, in grief, depressed, angry, agitated, aggressive, or fearful, I silently ask God to help that person. If all empaths were to do this, think how different the world would be!

Those with this capacity have the ability to know when someone is struggling, even if the other person is wearing their happy mask. If we choose to, we can silently 'call in' assistance from a higher place. Whether the help we request is Divine, Angelic, Spiritual or Universal it is requested from a place of heart, a place of love. However, if we chose not to intercede on their behalf, we still need to identify the emotion as not being our own and to disconnect from it.

To help me feel grounded I have to consistently pay attention to my own feelings. I have had to learn to name my emotions. This can be a new process for those who tend to spend so much time in the energy of others. We have to learn about our own feelings. I frequently tune in with myself and ask if what I'm feeling is in proportion to the events of my day? Has something happened since I got out of bed to make me feel this sad, or this tired or this angry? If these feelings are mine, I can deal with them while remaining solidly grounded in my own energy.

If they are not mine, I silently ask for Divine assistance for the person or situation I am picking up on. When I have finished praying, I ask to be disconnected and to return to my own energy. At this point I believe my job is done. There is nothing to be gained by remaining in a copy of the other person's pain for a second longer. By disconnecting I get to be me again, my own unique person, living my life.

In Ireland we go to funerals to sympathise with the family even if we don't know them that well. When the community takes the time to line out with the bereaved it is seen as an act of solidarity. In other countries funerals are often only attended by family and close acquaintances.

I was seven when I attended my first funeral – of the grandmother of a girl in my school year. At the funeral I felt lots of emotions. I now have a better understanding of these feelings than I did as a seven-year-old. I was anxious and curious about seeing my first real dead person! I was surprised how sad and upset I felt when I shook hands with my class-mate, Siobhan. I now know that I was in a copy of her energy and was feeling her sadness.

As a teenager, funerals had not got any easier for me. I cried so much as I queued to meet the family that eventually I stopped going. Now, while travelling to a funeral, I pray for assistance for all those in grief that I am going to meet. I then ask to remain in my own energy. I can now sympathise with the family. I can make eye contact and behave emotionally appropriate to my relationship with the mourners and the deceased. I now stay strong and grounded within my own energy.

In an earlier chapter, Understanding Sensitivity, I spoke about my meeting with the flustered manager. That day, once I realised that I was in his energy, I said a silent prayer for him and watched as he became calmer and grounded. We went on to have a very productive meeting.

When we know that we have to go into an emotionally challenging environment, we can ask for assistance for all those we are going to meet before we even get there. For example, before I go to visit anyone in hospital, prior to arriving I ask for assistance for all those I am going to meet who are in distress. I also include the words "and are open to receiving Divine assistance" as it's not for me to force help on those who do not wish to be helped. Having done this, I can remain solid in my own energy. As a result, I do not pick up on the pain or distress of the patients. This way the patient I am visiting is getting the best of me. I am able to chat comfortably. I know that my visit is of benefit to them, whereas crying or being emotional in their company will only add to their distress.

To be the healthiest and happiest we can be, we need to disconnect from the emotional copies of others as quickly as possible. When meeting clients, I feel their physical pain. I feel their injuries and illness as if it were mine. I do this briefly, to identify where in their body needs help. Then I immediately step out of the copy of their pain and step fully back into my own feelings. By continuing to remain in copies of the emotions and physical pain of others, we can become ill.

In the past I have held onto pains and aches, I have limped around my home, taken pain killers for headaches that were not mine and gone for naps even though I wasn't tired. A woman who attended one of my workshops, had the sudden realisation that her depression had started when she took on the job of carer to a recently widowed elderly woman. Her client was difficult to motivate and just wanted to stay in bed all day, though physically was well enough to get up and self-care.

We can become unpredictable and hard to be with. If our emotions and moods are affected by the people we meet as we go about out daily tasks, our partners and loved ones never know what to expect from us. If we go into the local grocery store in our own energy and come back out in a copy of the energy of whoever we met in there, how could anyone live with us? It can be challenging to live with a teenager who is going through hormonal changes. However, if we are seemingly changing personality, going from happy to sad, or angry and short-tempered without any apparent catalyst, we can spend large portions of our lives acting like a hormonal teenager.

We can become disempowered. If we meet someone who is in the depts of depression, we can take on a copy of their depression. Then there are two of us in that dark space. The longer we stay in that dark hole the more it feels like it's ours, the less energy we have, the less joy and hope we feel. The person we have taken on a copy of, can seek medical help or find a way of dealing with their despair, leaving us still in the darkness. When we pick up on depression, the sooner we identify that it is not ours the better. By doing the steps, (which I explain in the chapter Seven Steps), we can return to our own energy and appropriately offer assistance. Alternatively, we can give the person the choice of whether or not they would like assistance.

We can become overinvolved in situations that are not ours to solve. When our family or friends tell us of their personal problems, we feel our own concern and on top of our feelings we put a copy of their worries. Now the problem feels like it is ours. Many of us take on issues and feel they are our responsibility to fix. Then days later we can find ourselves trying to extricate ourselves from a situation that was never ours to begin with. Meanwhile, our family member or friend has come to depend on us as their go to person who solves their problems.

We could be encouraging them to find their own solution and offering them an ear for them to talk it through with. Instead, they may learn to depend on us to fix it for them. In doing this we are not fixing the problem. At best, we are temporarily mending it. We may be disempowering them by taking their life lessons from them. We can stop them from developing the skills to solve their own problems and thus take from their personal growth, and their feelings of personal empowerment.

I have a friend, Jane, who has what I call *ostrich syndrome*. A serial procrastinator, head in the sand, avoid the urgent issue as long as possible and find other things to fill the day. Last summer she was really behind on a project.

Being a typical empath, I offered to help. For the first three days we worked hard - starting many different tasks but completed nothing. By the end of day three we had very little to show for all our hard work.

I was running a workshop the following week and I really needed to get notes organised for it. On returning from Jane's house every day, instead of getting on with what I needed to do, I took to doing housework, clearing out cupboards, sorting old invoices, everything except preparing for the workshop. Thankfully, by day three I realised I had been repeatedly stepping into, and remaining in, a copy of Jane's energy.

I am pretty organised and generally deal with tasks in order of priority. For those three days I had avoided my own most important task. I went through my steps to disconnect from her energy and got organised for my workshop. The next day at Jane's I offered to work on one task. I calmly stuck at this one thing until it was completed. By staying in my own calm energy, I achieved more than in the previous three days combined. As I completed the agreed task, I noticed that Jane had also became more centred. Observing the structured way in which I was working, she was able to follow suit.

Sometimes it may seem beneficial to remain in the energy of others. Recently, before one of my client's arrived, I got into a super-efficient mode. I sorted out paperwork, evicted some spiders and their webs, puffed up cushions and dusted down the hallway. All this I accomplished in thirty minutes. I had met this client before and knew that she was an extreme housekeeper, who worked quickly and efficiently, leaving no possibility of dust. I knew I was in her energy. After she left, I was about to ruthlessly commence clearing out my kitchen cupboards. I really had to convince myself that I should disconnect from her and resume working at my own pace.

Another client, Sarah, told me how when she is feeling down, she intentionally seeks out her good-humoured friend to meet up with or to chat with by phone. Sarah knowingly takes on a copy of her friend's good humour. This may seem like the perfect solution but it does not allow Sarah to be honest and address her own feelings. Instead, she is intentionally putting on a copy of happy while leaving her own sadness buried. She has developed this as a tool over the years. A tool that means she can avoid painfully moments in her own life or at least postpone them. Instead of finding her voice and speaking up for herself every time her partner disrespects her, she phones her friend and takes on a copy of her good humour.

Sometimes it can be much more serious when we step into a copy of energy that is not ours. The following story shared by Tina shows how without warning we can drop into a place of hopelessness and depression.

THE BLACK HOLE

TINA

I woke up on a Wednesday morning and instantly knew I was feeling low, which being honest was kind of weird for me. I packed the kids off to school and decided to go out to the garden which normally helps to lift my spirits. No such luck this day, however. I had an appointment in town at 12 and headed off, even though it was the last thing I wanted or needed. I moped into it and when I came out, I had a missed call from Bríd. Normally I would return it in a jiffy but this time I didn't. I really wasn't up to speaking with anyone. When I got home, I headed back out to the garden.

About a half hour later the phone dinged, it was Bríd, by text this time. So, I read the text and she said she was picking up on my brother's energy. Now you see my brother is an alcoholic and with that there is lots of drama. I have learned with Bríd's help to detach. I love him dearly but this is his lesson to learn and I cannot help him. I've done all I can do and now it's up to him.

When I read this message, I was curious so I called Bríd not knowing what I would be told. She immediately asked me how I was. Before I had finished telling her, she told me I was in my brother's energy. She said that he was in a black hole and saw no way out and I was connected to his energy. Honestly, I was gobsmacked, because that was how I felt, so low, no way out, nearly like I was in the depts of depression.

Bríd and I both took a moment to ask for help for him and she then helped me to disconnect from his energy. I was kind of cross at myself for being in his energy. Bríd explained that without being aware, we can, at times slip very easily into the energy of family members. I was so glad of Bríd's help that day and am continuously learning while at the same time expanding my awareness.

THE DOMINO EFFECT

I consider empathic ability to be a part of our DNA, though this may not be acknowledged from a scientific viewpoint. For it to be a part of our genetics we must have inherited it from somewhere, or more accurately from someone. They have a saying in the Midlands "You didn't lick it off the ground" and so it is with our special ability. Therefore, it has to have come from our father or our mothers' side (or both). If we follow this thought on, it implies that we had relatives in previous generations who were also impacted by the emotions of others. As with all inherited genetics, no one is an exact replica of anyone else but if you have siblings, cousins, aunts, uncles, etc, chances are that some of these also have a version of your gift. If you are a parent your child may be an empath.

This is a gift that we will struggle to master. Even then, there will be times when we will unknowingly slip into the emotion or personality of others. We are very fortunate to live in this era. There is so much information available to us. Entire sections in libraries and book shops are dedicated to alternative literature. There are so many methods and items that we can immerse ourselves in as we seek the relevant information and assistance.

From items such as crystals, pendulums, meditation music, angel cards to books, workshops and internet talks on all these topics.

One of our challenges is the opposite to that of previous generations. We are challenged with somehow finding our way through the myriad of options to locate the information that is specific to our unique needs.

Thankfully, we live in a society where we are generally encouraged to be true to ourselves. Looking back to our ancestors and the times they lived in, that was not their reality. When my grandfather was a child, he told his mother that he was seeing *things*. She went to the local priest for advice. The priest duly visited their house and did his very best to physically beat it out of the child. The priest did not succeed, of course, as a gift cannot be beaten out of anyone! We may choose not to use it, but we still have the ability.

My grandfather went on to develop the ability to prophesy and to break curses. He learnt to become much more selective in who he shared this knowledge with. After his death I heard stories from neighbours of how, as a young man, he had told their parents that people would one day be buying bottles of water, which his neighbours had scoffed at. He also described large boxes that people would have in their parlours with a wire running up by the chimney onto the roof. In this box there would be a glass cover with changing pictures and families would gather at night to watch it. This was also scoffed at, but in a good-humoured way. These same neighbours knew that if they were to be victims of curses or phiseog (old superstitions) this would be the man they would be depending on to remove the hex.

Some of us may discover relatives on our family tree that were admitted to mental institutions. Were they empaths? Were they stepping into the emotions of others, taking on a copy of someone else's depression or anxiety and not able to disconnect? When we get to a point in our lives where we master our special ability, we can then finally accept it as a gift. A gift that often felt heavy as it passed down through the generations. I now proudly carry this torch and pray that as it passes down through future generations that the weight they carry will be much lighter.

When we have more than one empath living together, we can experience what I refer to as the 'domino effect'. This is when we pick up on something and then another empath picks up on it from us. Last year I had a phone call from a mother who was very concerned about the changes in her daughter's behaviour. Her daughter had recently become very anxious and they both had been unable to identify what had happened to cause such a change. They arrived as arranged on the Saturday morning for the appointment. The mum sat in the waiting area and I welcomed Laura to join me in my treatment room.

I start every session by inviting my client to light a candle and silently set their intention for what they would like to receive from the appointment. That day I took the candle from Laura and went to place it on the shelf. As I did so, I dropped it. While it was falling towards the wooden floor, I tried frantically to catch it. Thankfully it landed facing up and somehow it was still alight. I don't normally drop things. I asked Laura's guides what was going on. The answer I got was very short. "*Twelve weeks.*" With this information I asked her had she been clumsy lately? She smiled as she recalled some of the things she had done of late, bumping into furniture, spilling milk, dropping her toast that morning. I asked her was anyone else being clumsy. Again, she reflected and smiling she said her mum had started dropping things and had put the cereal in the fridge that morning. This was not normal for her mother either, who was usually very calm and efficient.

I then asked Laura what had changed in their lives and especially in her mother's life in the last twelve weeks. She told me that mum had started dating again and had met someone new. I asked her to describe his personality. Laura said John seemed very nice but was distracted and frequently clumsy. He didn't seem to be able to concentrate. There was a lot going on for him with his ex-wife and he had a legal situation coming up. She knew he was really anxious, though he never let on. I asked her how she knew he was anxious. She replied she didn't know how she knew, but she just felt it!

Laura is an empath, as is her mother. Her mum was picking up on John's energy and not disconnecting. Laura was picking up on her mother's new energy and not disconnecting. I then picked up on Laura's new energy and quickly disconnected. As we looked at her anxiety, we realised that this was also not hers. I taught her my seven steps and helped her to disconnect. Laura left my home that day solid in her own energy and ready to re-immerse herself in her normal teenage life.

When we get caught up in other people's problems and emotions, instead of helping the other person we can add to the problem, or we can even become the problem! We behave and speak from a place that is not one hundred percent ours. Our time can go into other people's situations and challenges and our own life lessons and dreams can be missed. In this situation Laura's anxiety had become her mother's total focus. So much so that she was unavailable to support John and unable to see how she was being affected.

*****

Have you ever an argument with a family member where for no apparent reason it got blown out of all proportion? This could also be the domino effect. Take a scenario where a mother and one of her children are both empaths. Mum, who is in a hurry, asks her two children to get in the car. Johnny refuses. Mum gets annoyed. Johnny becomes more defiant. Mum is now even more frustrated. Johnny has a full-on tantrum and is struggling to get his words out. Mum is now raising her voice and getting really angry. The situation has escalated out of all proportion.

Mum is in a copy of her son's energy, which she has put on top of her own stress. The child is picking up on his mother's energy and is adding it to his. The mother is then picking up on the child's new energy, which now includes a copy of her original energy and so it gets bigger and bigger. Each copy now includes the new copy as it continues to multiply.

Johnny has an older sister who, in his view, always gets what she wants. On this particular evening she had dictated what TV programme they watched. Johnny's favourite programme has just started when their mother asks them to get in the car. His sister starts laughing at him as she knows he won't get to see his programme. He is feeling disappointed, less valued, less important, feeling that his needs and his wishes are never heard. He knows there is no point saying to his mother that "Marie is being mean" as his mother won't hear him.

Picture the mother and son putting on extra sweaters as they put on layers of each other's energy and then layers of each other's new energy until the situation is ready to erupt. ×It becomes like a math's equation:

Johnny = undervalued + upset + disappointed

Mother = stressed + burdened

Then the empaths add in the other person's energy

Johnny = undervalued + upset + disappointed + *stressed + burdened*

Mother = stressed + burdened + **undervalued + upset + disappointed**

Then it starts to escalate

Johnny = (undervalued + upset + disappointed + *stressed + burdened)* **× 2**

Mother = (stressed + burdened + **undervalued + upset + disappointed)** × 2

Their emotions continue to escalate exponentially.

Johnny = (undervalued + upset + disappointed + *stressed + burdened)* **× 3**

Mother = (stressed + burdened + **undervalued + upset + disappointed)** × 3

Mum erupts and reprimands Johnny. Her good girl Marie is sitting quietly in the car. Johnny is emotionally drained and still feeling undervalued, upset and disappointed as well as holding copies of his mother's stress. He is not equipped to disconnect from the domino effect that he has just experienced and is still crying as he gets in the car. Mum having erupted has let off steam and returns to her normal energy. She joins her children and commences her journey.

When a parent reaches an understanding of their gift, they can then start to explain it to their children. This will help prevent situations getting out of hand and improve family relationships.

THE PSYCHIC CODE

We are each living unique lives. Not all will be healers, nor are we all meant to be. No man is an island and so each will have interactions with other people as we go about our daily lives. We can find ways to put these gifts to good use. If, for example, you are a teacher you will possibly be aware of the emotions of your students despite the mask they choose to wear. You may feel their sadness or anxiety without being told. With this knowledge perhaps you will make different decisions in your interactions with these students. Similarly, if you are a nurse, doctor, dentist, social worker or therapist you will have a better understanding of your patient. Whatever your walk of life, this gift can be used in a positive way, giving you a better understanding of your friends, work colleagues, employees, clients, customers and more importantly your family members.

In my work as a spiritual healer, I have learned to incorporate my abilities to guide me to my clients' physical, emotional and spiritual blocks. I then channel healing to those areas. Before I meet my clients, I take a few minutes and scan my body. I look for any pain or sensation that is not mine. I know that any new pains or sensations I now feel in my own body relate to the person I am about to meet. By noticing a new pain in my back or knee, I know that my next client has a pain in their back or knee. I use this information in my work to direct healing to these areas in the client's body. I ask their guides to show me what emotional issues need to be discussed and released. I may be shown images from their childhood, or their adult life. I may be shown if the person has been in a difficult or abusive relationship. While watching these images, I will tune in to how I am feeling as this is really my indication as to how the client was impacted as they went through these events.

I pay attention to any tension I am holding anywhere in my body and ask their spirit guides to explain. For example, I have felt weight on my shoulder as I looked at a picture in my mind's eye of the client holding tightly to a younger sibling. Occasionally I feel like I am being pulled in two different directions as if I am in the middle of a tug-of-war. I will ask the guides "Who am I being pulled between?" The answer is usually the client's parents. I might feel like I am walking on eggshells and again I will ask the guides "Who it is that makes the client feel uncomfortable? Who makes them feel they have to watch everything they say?"

In addition to the images, pains and sensations, I also observe my behaviour. Am I able to sit and relax or am I constantly getting up to fix things? Are the positions of the cushions annoying me? Am I looking for cobwebs and for things that need cleaning? Has my energy suddenly dropped? Am I just staring at the wall and not able to see the beautiful day that is unfolding outside the window? Am I self-conscious about my image, thinking I should check my hair, or change my clothes? All these insights help me to understand and help my client.

My own workspace is quite tidy, it gets a quick once over every morning before I start work. I have developed my gift in such a way that as I look around my room before the client arrives, I am looking as if through their eyes. I am learning that they are perhaps self-critical, have low energy, or lack enthusiasm for life. They see what needs to be done rather than seeing all that they have achieved. Or they are unable to relax. As I identify these traits, I again ask their guides to show me why the client behaves like this, and what are the belief systems behind this behaviour. Armed with this information I discuss these images with the client. This gives them a better understanding of themselves and they start to release that which no longer serves them.

However, sometimes I forget that I am in their energy and not my own. While awaiting their arrival I may find myself running off to do house chores. On one occasion,

I kept changing my clothes, feeling I didn't look good enough and that no matter what I put on, it didn't look right. Thankfully, by the third change I realised this was the client's energy I was in and not mine!

Of the empaths I have met many seem to have more than one psychic gift, thus adding to their struggle to understand themselves. It's possible that everyone has some level of psychic capability, where they will have had moments of knowing or an awareness without any logical explanation. Many will have no understanding of how to use their gifts and may not be aware that these abilities can be switched on and switched off. This is not something to be feared, it is just a part of our DNA. It has been passed down to us from previous generations. I consider these gifts to be an integral part of who I am.

There are seven recognised ways in which we can use our senses to receive psychic information. It's important to note that information received psychically can relate to the past, present or to the future. Each of us will interpret it in our own unique way. In everyday life some people's senses may be stronger than others. There are those who have perfect 'twenty-twenty' vision, or those with excellent hearing, perhaps you have a strong sense of taste or smell. It's the exact same with psychic abilities.

Clairalience	**(smell)**
Clairaudience	**(hearing)**
Clairgustance	**(taste)**
Clairsentience	**(sixth-sense)**
Clairtangence	**(touch)**
Clairvoyance	**(sight)**
Clairempathy	**(emotional sensation)**

Clair is the French word for clear.

Clairalience:

The ability to receive psychic information through sense of smell.

If you have this gift, you are able to use scent as a medium through which a message is relayed. This might be perfume, or cigarettes, flowers or any other smell.

On entering my treatment room one day prior to a new client's arrival I was shocked by the horrible smell that greeted me. The only smell I could associate it with was someone with very bad flatulence. I was mortified as it was a new client that I was expecting and was

46

concerned she would think it was me that had the problem. As soon as she arrived, I quickly explained about scent evidence. She started to laugh and then informed me that her granny had terrible wind. She went on to explain that all family gatherings include their stories about their granny's flatulence. As children they would argue over who would have to accompany her shopping or to attend church. Not only did granny have an issue with wind she also had a wicked sense of humour. The family had so many hilarious stories about their beloved grandmother. The client took comfort knowing that her granny was around and that she would have got a laugh out of my mortification.

When you get a subtle smell that you cannot associate with anything in your surrounding area, ask yourself where is it coming from. If there isn't a logical explanation then it's a message. The woman in the following story does just that.

AIR FRESHENER

ANN O'GRADY

Last summer while on holidays in the USA, I visited some relatives in Connecticut. I stayed in an awful hotel (it was conveniently located close to my relatives who are elderly, so it was easy for me to walk to their house).

My main memory of this hotel was the awful smell of air freshener, really not a pleasant smell. Anyway, I visited my relatives and completed the rest of my stay in America.

Fast forward four or five months. My holiday is long forgotten and I am back at work. One Wednesday morning as I am driving to work, I get the smell, then when I go to my work place the smell is still there. It took me a little while to realise that it was the smell of the awful air freshener in the hotel in America.

As I have mentioned, I noticed the smell on Wednesday morning, but by Friday it was with me all the time, so I decided to ring my relative in Connecticut that evening when I got home from work. My relative was delighted I phoned, because only a few days ago he had had a terrible fall and had sustained injuries and was very shaken by the whole experience. This poor gentleman got the medical assistance he needed, but had no one to talk to about his experience and I was delighted to be able to speak to him in his time of need.

Clairaudience:

The ability to hear messages from the spiritual or angelic realms.

People with this gift will receive their psychic information through their hearing. They will have the power to hear sounds that exist beyond the ordinary experience of others. They may hear the voices of the deceased or perhaps hear messages from the angelic realm. For some the information will come in a subtler manner. They may experience a loved one's song coming on the radio when thinking of them. Craig is one of these people with this ability.

SONGS FROM ANOTHER PLACE

CRAIG DAVEY

I have always had a sense of words of songs and lines of poetry and prose that stick in my head and would play all day. I didn't really give them too much attention outside of just being aware of them. While attending one of Bríd's workshop groups I learnt a lot more about how we can receive psychic information. One of these was clairaudience (I think it is called). The sense of having a communication from another time or place, of a spiritual world level of existence that can communicate with you in this way.

In the last few months, I have become more aware of this ability. An example of this would be that recently I just woke up and I had the song "Islands in the Stream" playing in my mind. There was no reason to trigger this song. I had not heard it on the radio recently or on TV or anything. I thought: "This is strange, this is interesting". It is a song by Kenny Rogers and Dolly Parton. My mum actually loved that song. It was one of her favourite songs, and it was just playing away in my thoughts all day there in the background. It would pop in every now and again.

That evening I switched on the news and found out that Kenny Rogers had passed away that day. To me, I think that gave me a sense that my mother was communicating to me that Kenny Rogers was in her spiritual realm now. Or it could have come from somewhere else in that realm I'm not sure. But it was just a sure sign of knowing that there is something else.

I am learning more and more to pay attention to these words, these lines, these songs in my mind when they just come in like that, completely unannounced. Just giving them space to reveal whatever they might be. So that was a very special gift to have from Bríd to know this and to give it the space to allow it to flower and find out a little bit more about it.

Clairgustance:

The ability to receive psychic information through taste.

This is the paranormal ability to taste a substance without putting anything in one's mouth. A teenage girl who came to see me explained that sometimes she gets a metallic taste in her mouth. She associates the taste with her granddad. He was a metal worker and spent much of his working life welding. It is a rare occurrence for her but generally happens when she is having difficult life experiences. It brings her a real sense of comfort to know that this man who she loved so much continues to watch over her. He is aware of her day-to-day life even though he is no longer physically present.

Clairsentience:

A strong gut instinct and the ability to perceive the emotions and pains of others.

Often labels can limit or pigeon-hole us. But sometimes, labels can be the keys to our freedom. In my thirties I went to a kinesiologist for an allergy test. On answering her questions, she suggested that I had clairsentient ability. This was a new word for me. She explained that a clairsentient person is aware of the feelings and worries of other people and has a strong 'gut' intuition. This was a label that resonated with me, as it explained so many of my life experiences that previously had made absolutely no sense. However, it was not until I accepted that I was also an empath that I fully understood what was happening to me. The clairsentient has an awareness of the emotions of others while the empath feels and assumes those emotions.

Clairsentients tend to be very intuitive. For some of us, the information we receive may be a gut feeling that someone can't be trusted, or maybe for no apparent reason we think we should take a different route to work.

Many people will have had unexplained moments of knowing who is on the phone before we answer it. You may have called unexpectedly to check on someone who, unknown to you on a rational level, was in difficulty.

Clairtangence:

The ability to receive messages by holding an object.

The word psychometry is also used to describe this ability. Those who have clairtangence ability receive psychic information when they physically touch a person, animal, or object. The information is not about the object itself but instead the object triggers information in relation to its owner or events connected to its owner from the past, the present or the future. Occasionally people with this gift assist law enforcement with locating missing persons or providing information in unsolved crimes.

Clairvoyance:

The ability to receive psychic messages through sight.

The word clairvoyant is probably the one we are most familiar with. People with this ability will see spirit or have had moments of thinking that they saw movement out of the corner of their eye, that no one else will have noticed. When some clairvoyants use their gift, they may see entire scenes as if watching a movie. Some will see the images with their eyes closed; some will clearly see spirit as distinctly as they see the living; others will just see an outline of a spirit.

Clairempathy:

The ability to feel the mental and or emotional state of another individual.

Those of us with this gift psychically feel the emotions and/or physical pain of others. Many with this gift can also feel geopathic energy, residual energy and soul energy which can adversely affect our health and wellbeing. I have included individual chapters on these three topics.

Having accepted these labels, I have added a few of my own. I started using the word healer but thought it didn't quite explain what I was doing. Spiritual healer is the title I work under. By tuning into the blocks in the lives of my clients, I create a space where these issues can be healed. Through Divine intervention I ask that their physical and emotional pains be released. All these labels are a part of who I am. None of them define me but they help me gain a better understand of who I am. I simply think of those who are psychic as having the ability to move from head thinking to gut thinking.

Over the years I have built up a log of what I refer to as my psychic code, listing the signs and symbols that I have been receiving. At first, they seemed very random and hard to decipher. Once a male client came to see me and as he sat down in the treatment room, I saw in my mind's eye a picture of a brick wall with a crack running through it. I asked him was he doing some building work? No. Was there a structural problem with his house? No. I couldn't put a context on the reference. I asked the guides for other information and got pictures of the man sitting in his kitchen at night-time with the lights off. Then I saw a picture of him in hospital. I discussed the images with him and channelled healing for him.

I forgot about the image and what it might mean until a week later when I was working with a female client. I had the same picture: that of a brick wall with a crack.

This time I knew what it was. I thought back to what was the main topic of conversation I had with the man a week earlier. That topic was all about the man having been through a mental break down. I had come to the information much later in the man's session. This time I knew straight away what the guides wanted me to focus on.

The more I paid attention to the signs and images the more I built up what I refer to as my personal psychic code. Similar to learning a new language, the greater the vocabulary and the more confident I am using this vocabulary then the smoother the conversation will be. Whether I am communicating with angels, guides or loved ones in the spirit realm, the more effort I have put in to learning their language the more informative and beneficial the conversation. I would suggest that if this is something you would like to do, then you simply start by paying attention to your senses. Write down when you get random smells, images, songs, colours, tastes, feelings, etc. Note what is happening in your life at these times or if something unusual happens for a loved one. You will gradually build up your own personal psychic code.

The decision to develop your psychic gifts, or not, is completely your choice. You can decide this at your own discretion. Whether or not we develop these abilities is not going to have a negative impact on our lives. I explain this as being similar to someone who is a very talented musician. They can decide never to play or they can occasionally play a few tunes at home. Alternatively, they may decide to practice once a week or they can dedicate their entire life to music.

However, unless we come to an understanding of our empathic ability it can have a detrimental effect on our health, wellbeing and relationships. Imagine a light switch working under normal circumstances. We turn it on as the room gets dark. Later that night we turn it off when we are leaving the room. If someone keeps flicking that switch on and off the bulb will blow. Likewise, if we are moving in and out of head thinking to gut thinking, or moving in and out of other people's energy without any controls in place, we can blow a fuse. Particularly if we are not even aware that we are doing it.

Generally, I use my psychic gifts during a prebooked appointment with a client. But this is not always the case. Sometimes my ability switches on when I least expect it. Knowing that we have the ability to switch from head thinking to gut thinking, without making a conscious decision to do so, it is very important that we take the time, daily, to protect and ground ourselves.

In 2017 I was doing some work in County Kerry. I took the opportunity to meet up with my friend Peter. It was a lovely spring day as we headed off for a drive along the coast. We stopped at Smerwick. I didn't know this part of the country at all and was happy to get out and explore. The area is not commercialised and we were the only ones there when we arrived. Peter stopped to take a phone call and I wandered on ahead.

As I started walking down the path, I had a strong feeling to climb over the wall and go to the right. As I walked down the hill the scene in front of me changed. Looking around me, it was as if I had travelled back in time. In the water I could see ships from another era but that was not where my gaze landed. On the shore were rows of men with their arms and legs bound. As they sat there helplessly, soldiers walked slowly among them. Looking closer at the men I could see their legs were damaged and some had limbs severed, yet these men sat quietly as their captives took their time to mutilate the bodies of their captives.

I had no idea what I was looking at. A few minutes earlier I was looking at an isolated green hill, and rocky shoreline. I struggled to adjust to this new image. I reminded myself that I did not need to understand the scene in order to bring healing. I asked for a passageway for any souls that were ready to transition to the light. I also asked for a white light to surround the area and release all residual energy held on the shore from the atrocities that had been carried out there.

When Peter joined me, I explained the psychic image to him. Thankfully, he has a vast historical knowledge. He knew that a Spanish mercenary army had surrendered here but didn't know the details. As soon as I completed the clearing work needed, we headed off to find a restaurant. I was very much in need of food and a strong pot of tea to ground myself and gather my thoughts.

While I was tucking in to my much-needed lunch, Peter looked up the details on the internet. In September 1580 a squadron of Spanish ships, manned by Italian and Spanish mercenaries had come to the assistance of the Irish Catholics in Munster in their efforts to rebel against English Protestant rule. On arrival, their ships were blockaded in the bay at Smerwick by the British. After a short battle the captain of the Catholic mercenary force decided to surrender to the English. He and those of higher rank were all granted safe passage in exchange for surrendering his men. The prisoners were offered that their life would be spared if they renounced their Catholic faith. On refusal, their arms and legs were severed or broken repeatedly by an ironsmith. They were left in agony for a day and a night and then hanged.

On reflection, I realised these men had achieved a small victory. None had cried out while being tortured thus withholding from their captors the satisfaction of hearing their cries.

BELIEFS

I believe in God. My belief is based on the example of my family and my own life experiences. It is for each of us to come to our own understanding, relationship and belief in a creator. Whether your beliefs are religious or spiritual, both are an understanding of something far greater than human love, a creator who is infinite love. If you have such a belief system, then you can ask this creator of infinite love to help you disconnect from all energy other than your own.

I have been fortunate, through my psychic abilities to have seen visions of Jesus, Our Lady and various saints. I have also seen Deities and Goddesses from other religious beliefs. Because of these visions and other experiences, it is easy for me to believe in a power outside of what most people experience in their daily lives. For me, this is just part of my everyday life. That said, the positive feedback I get from clients also reassures me that I am using my gifts as intended.

COMFORT AND NURTURING

KAREN

My life has changed for the better since meeting Bríd. I had just begun down a new path I was very unsure of.

From the moment our session began, the comfort and nurturing I experienced made things all the clearer. I worried less about the future, and the connections I made helped me understand the past. Since my session I have been able to settle in the present and trust that things will only get better. And they have!

My health has improved. I'm no longer on medication. My studying is improving and my new business is growing every week.

Becoming more self-aware has caused a positive ripple effect in my home, family and life in general. Meeting Bríd has shown me how to be present and calm. Her spirit has inspired me to allow mine to grow and evolve. Bríd is truly beautiful and a great blessing to us all.

More often than not, the healing my clients receive in their session is not visible instantly. I don't always get to see the results or hear back from the clients. I have learnt to let people go from my thoughts when the treatment ends and I picture myself handing them back to God. Over time, I have learnt to trust in the process of the healing power available and I am blessed with a strong belief in the power of prayer.

On other occasions the impact is immediate and visible to all. This was the case in the following story. However, even though the result was immediate I did not see it, as the person requesting the healing was at the other side of the world. When I got the request for help, I simply trusted in the power of prayer.

REMOTE HEALING FROM ACROSS THE ATLANTIC

ANONYMOUS

Prior to going on holiday, I had an infection in the nailbed of my finger. I had been treating it and taking care of it before travelling. But a day or so after the flight, the infection was getting visibly worse and travelling down the finger. My fellow companions urged me to seek medical assistance. I knew too that I was in trouble.

Being away from home, I thought of Bríd. I contacted Bríd and asked her to channel healing remotely for me. She prayed for healing. The following day I noticed the throbbing easing and the infection improving in my finger. Within a few days my finger had healed remarkably. My travelling companions couldn't get over the healing that they witnessed. Bríd truly is a wonderful, gifted healer and one of God's Earth angels. I feel blessed to know her.

Last year, I went to visit Kitty, a woman in her early nineties at her home in Limerick. She was bed ridden and was struggling to accept the aging process. Her niece had asked me to visit their home in order to help her find acceptance and peace of mind as she approached the end of her time in this life. As I chatted with Kitty, I could see her mother's spirit sitting on a chair by the foot of her bed. I described this spirit to Kitty. I remember that I was surprised at how tall her mother was, nearly six foot, whereas the woman I was channelling for was barely five foot. As Kitty's mother's spirit sat patiently waiting,

I could see her in my mind's eye doing beautiful lace needle work. I then saw the spirit of Kitty's husband standing at the other side of the bed. He kept fidgeting with his hearing aid and his foot was tapping. Running happily around his feet was a small brown and white terrier.

On describing all that I had seen, the elderly woman sat up in bed. Crying happy tears, she confirmed that these were indeed accurate descriptions of her mother, her husband and their little dog. Kitty then grasped my hand asking She had spent her life living in blind faith. She had grown up in a period where it wasn't acceptable to question religious beliefs. Whatever was preached on the pulpit was accepted without question. This woman had learnt to say her prayers and to hope for the best. It was an honour for me to see the peace and acceptance that came over her as she let go her fears of dying and instead looked forward to being reunited with those she loved.

On my drive home I reflected on how many people live in 'blind faith' and how fortunate I am. It is very easy for me to have complete belief in the existence of God when I get to see so many extraordinary visions and having witnessed miracles.

One client who I have had the privilege of meeting on a number of occasions is Mary, who was raised in America by her Irish parents. She has an open heart and mind and is steadfast in her belief in a loving God. Through her sessions she has come to a clearer understanding of what issues are hers to work on and which are not hers. She has been able to give permission to her loved ones to come to their own understandings and to take responsibility for their own actions.

EMOTIONAL AND SPIRITUAL HEALING

MARY CLARE MCGRATH

Every year I live in County Clare, Ireland for the months of spring. One of the reasons I see Bríd, is because each time I'm there I am seeking emotional and spiritual healing. I grew up in an alcoholic home. I know I have blind spots in my thinking and in my behaviour, as a result of that early formation.

I believe God wants me to heal. I want to heal, as well. Each time I see Bríd, she helps me to understand ways in which my thinking and behaviour can change to continue healing.

I believe her gifts of knowing, seeing and sensing are gifts from a loving God. I have made significant changes based on things Bríd brings to my attention. My visits to her strengthen my belief in a loving God that seeks an intimate connection with me.

For me, my belief in a God of love is the single most important reason that I am able to function. Otherwise, being an empath would be crippling and debilitating. My beliefs have taught me to let go my fears and understand that the world is not mine to fix.

There are many times when I have to accept that a bigger power is at play. We may not understand what is going on but if we have an understanding of a God whose energy is love then we can trust our gut and follow our intuition.

With our belief system and a greater understanding of our empathic abilities, we are able to trust in our God and trust the process, instead of ignoring all the signs that we are being given in our dreams or through our senses. On occasion the signs can seem incredible, so much so that we cannot share them with anyone else out of fear of not being believed or being ridiculed. We may try to discard them and convince ourselves that they did not happen and "I must have imagined it." The more we can open up and acknowledge the signs, even if we don't understand them at the time, the stronger our spiritual connection will become.

PEGASUS

CRAIG DAVEY

When I was young, around about eight years of age I think, but I can't be sure, I went to the zoo with my family and friends. While there I remember looking up and seeing a Pegasus flying in the sky and then it disappeared behind what I remember as some kind of a mountain, which obviously wasn't there either.

Years later, when I was in my teenage years, one of my mum's friends, Violet, who had been at the zoo with us, was visiting our home and she said to me "Craig do you remember the time we saw the flying horse when you were younger?" I was astonished. I said, "Did you see it too?" and she said, "Yea I did, do you remember we saw it?" which for me was just incredible.

Since then, throughout my life, on numerous occasions I have had the Pegasus symbol come up in different situations. I can't remember all of them. But one I do remember, which sounds quite strange, was connected to my mum's passing. She and I were very, very, close. She had cancer, and my wife and I looked after her at home. She passed away at our house. Prior to this we had borrowed a bed from the hospital that she had used downstairs. That day after her remains had been removed by the undertaker, we striped the bed completely and found a huge Pegasus symbol covering the whole of the mattress. I hadn't realised it was a Pegasus bed and there was the symbol. Seeing the symbol gave me comfort.

Not related to what I had seen at the zoo or anything, my mum wore a cardigan in those final weeks. She had the cardigan for a while but she wore it a lot those days. She had a Pegasus brooch that she had seen somewhere and liked and bought and she wore this brooch on the cardigan.

It happened again when I bought Bríd first book. I was looking through it and one of the first things I saw when I turned to the back cover was that it was published by Pegasus Publications. This to me felt like a sign that it was the right book for me to read.

Other times in my life, at different significant events, there would be the Pegasus symbol, again just on mundane objects, but very symbolic for me. I am not sure exactly what it symbolises but it is special. It gives me the feeling that wherever I see it there is a sense of presence. It connects me back to that other realm of bigger things and a knowing outside of the everyday. It makes me feel that I am, to a certain extent, still linked to my mum and to a spiritual presence.

The people who seek me out are open to the possibility that there's something more than what is visible. I say to these people "If you believe in a higher power then why not ask that power for help?" We are all on our own journey. By consciously including an awareness of God in our day-to-day activities and asking for assistance in our daily struggles, our journey can be smoother. The more comfortable we are in our beliefs, the more open we are to accepting others and their beliefs.

"If a man reaches the heart of his own religion,

he has reached the heart of the others too."

Mahatma Gandhi

RULES AND EXPECTATIONS

From the time we are born, to the time we die, we are told to follow the rules. From our very first breath on this planet there are rules. First, there are hospital rules; rules on delivery procedures, feeding times, visiting times, who can visit the new-born baby and how many visitors. Someone decides if our siblings are allowed visit us. Our mothers are instructed on feeding times, how to hold us, how to change us, how often to wash us, and all the while advertisements tell the new mum what products to use.

Different countries have different procedures, different rules and expectations for the new mothers to follow. Some young mums can be made to feel as though they are failures if they are unable to breast feed, while in other countries it is considered the norm to use formula. There can be pressure to have a 'natural' delivery and not to use drugs to ease the pain of contractions. There are perceptions of the perfect child that sleeps through the night and only cries twice a day.

Before our first day on the planet is completed, many of us have a chart and baby book to measure our size,

72

weight, length, height and development. This book now accompanies us on our journey home and we get to be assessed and judged as we grow. We are weighed and measured regularly and our responses checked. Our movement is monitored and the timing of our first tooth is recorded. Mothers are asked questions on when did we lift our heads on our own, speak our first word, crawl and take our first steps. The doctors and nurses check for any defects, delay in development, under nourishment, underweight, overweight etc.

The pressure on parents increases as they strive to achieve perfection, not just with their offspring and parenting skills, but also to conform to society's image of the perfect family. Parents will add their own goals of what they want to achieve, determined not to repeat any perceived errors in the way they were raised by their parents. Those of us who are sensitive to energy can feel the stress of our mothers as they jump through hoops for the various health agencies. While all the baby wants is to sleep, be fed, cleaned and loved. Sometimes between the health agencies and medical staff performing their duties to assess us they can miss the fact that all babies are perfect. We are each unique and we are each perfect, even if we do not quite tick all their boxes.

Many new mothers struggling with lack of sleep, as they adjust to the responsibility of being carers to a new life, can feel added stress from society. How long after giving birth should it take to return to the perfect weight and figure? All their body wants to do is to curl up and go to sleep? Their parenting skills can also come under judgment from their family members, in-laws, friends, cultural beliefs, TV and magazines. The do's and don'ts of perfect parenting are endless. The list of rules may seem insurmountable at times. All this while we are still in nappies!

Likewise, for new fathers, now expected to prove their new age skills: provider, hunter, gatherer, mixed with sensitive, gentle and caring. Without explanation or training Dad should know how to hold, feed, change and engage with his new dependent. Same sex and single parents may feel all the more under the microscope of society as they work to prove they are worthy of the task of parenting.

As we grow the rules keep coming - rules of the land, of the road, etiquette and class rules, cultural, religious, house rules, school, club, rules for various sporting organisations and so on. Sometimes the rules conflict and rules can change. Today's rules and tomorrow's rules may not be the same. Today, in most countries, women can vote and can remain in their employment after they marry. Once this would have been unthinkable. Up until recently in Ireland divorce and same sex marriage were not allowed.

In some countries the rules of the road tell us to drive on the left, others tell us to drive on the right. When city driving, we may turn down a lane that has always been two-way traffic to discover it is now a one-way and we may even get a ticket because we have broken the rules. Speeding limits on parts of the road change, again resulting in possible tickets and fines. Different parking meters allow us varying amounts of time, this too can change. Sometimes, as the new rules replace the old rules, they can cause conflict and confusion.

I had an interesting conversation on this topic with a Native American. He commented on the similarities between our two cultures and how we had adapted to Christianity. He noticed in Ireland we have held on to some of our pagan beliefs and merged them into our new religion. For example, in rural Ireland many of us still put out the May Branch on the eve of May 1st to ward off *bad fairies and goblins* while at the same time we dedicate the month of May to Mary, Mother of Jesus.

He recounted his grandmother's stories on how their people traded their beliefs for Christianity and food. Their culture held tales of the Thunder Bird. During storms it would swoop down unseen from the skies and capture animals and sometimes even people in its massive talons, taking them away to another world. They believed that thunder, was the sound of their massive wings beating against their bodies. He recalled as a young child being made to get out of bed by his grandmother to pray the rosary during a particularly bad storm to protect them from the Thunder Bird. As the storm raged over head, his grandmother led them in frantic recitals of the rosary for protection from this mythical bird. Even though she was now a Christian she still believed in the old customs of her people.

As an adult it can be hard to accept that things you were told, and believed, all your life are in fact wrong. For many children, the effort involved in trying to understand the rules can be overwhelming. Again, add into this confusion that so many of us are sensitive and feel the confusion of others struggling to understand the rules, or sometimes fighting against the changes to the rules.

I started primary school just before my fourth birthday. The first two classes, baby class and senior infants, as they were then called, were not too strict but yet they had rules. When the bell rings you go in. When the bell rings you go out. You don't talk and you sit on a chair all the time you are in the class-room; you ask for permission to go to the bathroom and you always do as you are told by the teacher.

A fortnight before my sixth birthday I started first class. Here we had homework, spellings and maths tables to learn, reading to practice and we were introduced to the Irish language with strange words to pronounce. Fridays were test days! Here again our progress and performance were measured but now with consequences. Any spelling or maths table we got wrong resulted in us being ridiculed, punished and slapped.

At the time, terms like sensitive, or special needs, dyslexia, ADD, ADHD, were not part of the system. Instead, the nun used terms like 'stupid', 'lazy' and 'idiot'. Every Friday resulted in numerous slaps for me, as I reversed my letters and got many of my spellings wrong in our weekly test, irrespective of how long I spent at home learning the spellings. I was in my twenties before I discovered that I had dyslexia. This word changed my view of myself and my belief of my intellect. Often, I had felt inferior and had believed that the names used by the nuns in my primary education, like 'dumb' and 'stupid' were true. The word dyslexic explained so much.

In first class I really couldn't understand what was happening. I would learn the spellings and then repeat the letters back to my mother on Thursday nights. On Friday mornings, as the nun called the word in the test, I would repeat it in my brain and then write it down. But even though I knew dog was D O G, which I had repeated over and over the night before and now repeated as I wrote it, feeling confident that I definitely had this one right, somehow, as if by magic, my pencil had written G O D. It seemed impossible, as no matter what I did I would get slapped.

Being stupid was not the worst crime you could be guilty of; you could be a 'leftie'. A leftie was anyone who wrote with their left hand. This apparently was a sign that you were in league with the devil. These children had it worse than I did because even if they got all of their spellings right, they still got slapped for writing with their left hand. It's hard to believe that a practicing catholic nun could still believe in such phiseog (old superstitious tales). Surprisingly, this seems to have been the case throughout much of Ireland as lefties had it beaten out of them. I would love to have asked *"Where do these children go to hang out with*

Satan?", as I wondered what he looked like. I had a feeling he might resemble someone I knew! Sometimes those tasked with enforcing the laws can have grey areas, mixing old rules and beliefs with new ones, thus creating additional confusion and consequences.

Then we were introduced to a new subject, Catechism. Each child was given a little square blue book which contained the basis of the catholic religion. We were tasked with learning this book verbatim.

Q. *"Who made the world?"* – A. *"God made the world."*

Q. *"Who created man?"* – A. *"God created man."*

And God help you if you didn't know the answer, worded it slightly differently, or gave a shorter version.

Next, we were introduced to the Ten Commandments:

1. I am the Lord, thy God. Thou shall not place other gods before me.

2. Thou shall not take the name of the Lord thy God in vain.

3. Keep holy the Lord's Day.

4. Honour thy father and thy mother.

5. Thou shall not kill.

6. Thou shall not commit adultery.

7. Thou shall not steal.

8. Thou shall not bear false witness.

9. Thou shall not covet thy neighbour's wife.

10. Thou shall not covet thy neighbour's goods.

As we prepared for our First Confession, we were given three commandments to learn verbatim each week. Then at the end of the month we had to be able to recite all ten. Bearing in mind the children in the class were generally between six and seven years of age, this was quite an achievement. This task was in addition to the dreaded weekly spelling and maths tests.

Now we were instructed to consider each commandment before our First Confession and make a list of our sins to tell the priest in the confessional. We were told to examine our conscience.

Wow, what did it all mean?

1. Apparently, we shouldn't worship dolls. Okay, that seemed logical.

2. Only use God's name while praying. This bothered me as I liked to chat to God in my mind, was this a sin?

3. Sunday was not a day of work and we must go to Mass. I lived on a small dairy farm and chores still had to be done. I asked my mum about this and she said chores were allowed.

4. Obey our parents.

5. Don't kill anyone. At six years of age this seemed unlikely, though I may have harboured dark thoughts on school test days.

6. Adultery – no idea, but I didn't think I had ever done it!

7. Don't steal.

8. Don't tell lies.

9. Don't covet your neighbour's wife – no idea but it sounded painful.

10. Don't covet your neighbour's goods – again, no idea.

What I found most confusing was the instruction to examine our conscience. I had no idea what a conscience was but I decided the nun must be talking about our homework journals. We were to see if we had committed any sins there. The nun used to tell me off when I would fail my tests as my homework journal indicated I had learnt my spellings. I decided she must think I was lying and wanted me to tell the priest this sin while in the confessional.

We were then given a list of sins we could use if we couldn't come up with any of our own.

I told a lie.

I didn't do something my mother told me to do.

I stole a cookie (the nun explained that a cookie was a biscuit and these were kept in cookie jars!)

I said a bad word.

Having gone through the commandments and examined my homework journal, I decided to lie, and tell the priest that "I told a lie." I hoped he wouldn't ask me what the lie was as I would have to lie further and make up a story. Thankfully he asked no questions and for this sin I was given three Hail Mary's as penance.

As I got older, more and more rules have been added to the list of do's and don'ts. I now try to live my life by two rules.

"Love the Lord your God with all your heart and with all your soul and with all your mind. This is the first and greatest commandment".

"Love your neighbour as yourself."

Matthew 22:37-40

Children need to know what the boundaries are. These need to be clear and consistent, and they need to be flexible in response to the individual child. They help create a safe environment in which children can grow and expand their independence. This is all the more so for sensitive children, who are already struggling to understand the emotions they are being bombarded with.

The following client's testimonial tells of a child's struggle to follow her father's inconsistent rules. She tells of the anxiety and stress caused by this struggle and how it affected her in her adult life. Thankfully she has been able to release this fear and now deals with each new situation without her childhood baggage.

DADDY'S HOUSE - DADDY'S RULES

MARIA

I decided to visit Bríd as I was at a point in my life where I felt I was at a 'crossroads'. My children were grown up. I was facing into the second part of my life where I had no excuses left but to start living for me.

My core issue was that I battled with unfocused anxiety and sometimes paranoia. I approached issues and people with an underlying fear of doing the wrong thing or causing upset. I had trained as a therapist so I had lots of personal therapy and also studied and reflected on many aspects of personal struggles and this had made me highly sensitive and aware of my emotions. Knowing a feeling like anxiety has no basis in any issue does not necessarily mean, for me, that it went away.

I spent years intellectualising why I was feeling the way I was, but that didn't make the anxiety go away. I suppose awareness isn't always enough to battle with a deep-seated emotion. It made me more understanding of myself, but it didn't stop the anxiety having a huge effect on my behaviour. I spent lots of time reflecting on conversations and interactions I had with others, feeling anxious that I had in some way done something wrong. I went around almost apologetic for my existence, always sensitive to the effect I was having on others, even my close family and friends. I was nice to everyone and yet neglectful of myself.

Spending time talking to Bríd I felt a connection that was more than a 'I understand what your feeling'. It was a deep affection and a feeling of safety not unlike what you may feel as a child being protected and safe with a parent. I opened up to her and felt it was okay to fall apart and be vulnerable and childlike. Therefore, the healing she subsequently did with me was with me being totally open and that's why I feel it was so effective.

Once the healing started, she worked on areas of my body that she felt needed healing. When the physical healing part of the session was over, she talked to me about seeing someone shouting at me with such force that they were spitting. That related to my father, who was a very angry man. From early childhood my home was a place of constant anxiety as I never knew what the rules were. One day I would do something and it would be fine. The next day I could do the same thing and I would be shouted at, or someone else would be, which frightened me too. I grew up being wary, afraid and anxious. Bríd focused on the anxiety that was now trapped in my stomach and said she thought that if we didn't work on releasing it, it could eventually make me ill.

I was very apprehensive about getting in contact with it, but because I felt so safe and trustful of Bríd, I risked the feelings that may surface. With her help, I allowed this thing, this trapped fear, to rise up into my throat and let go. It came out as a guttural painful sound, but I also tasted some kind of metallic substance. It's hard to relate it to a specific taste. I don't know how long it lasted but once it ended, I felt dizzy and light-headed but also emotionally like I had let something go, a freedom from a heavy weight.

Since that time, I have felt so much better. I have what, to me, seems an almost reckless attitude to things now. Not in a dangerous or destructive way, but I feel free to do things without that crippling anxiety, nobody is going to shout at me, and if they do, I will deal with it as an adult, not as a scared child. I still default back to the anxiety when I am tired, but it's not deep seated, it's just a habit that I can now let go of without indulging in hours of unfounded anxiety.

What has also happened is that I am much more caring of myself. I really felt the childhood fear and feel so protective of myself now, knowing that I have carried this fear for so long and that it's now safe for me to look after myself and not spend all my energy being protective in case I get shouted at. I now enjoy things and people and laugh and let go of things and no longer take everything so seriously.

I am not afraid if people don't like me or agree with me. It's part of life, but I *feel* that now, which is a much deeper *knowing* than knowing it in my head.

I am so grateful for the time Bríd spent with me, because she was truly there for me and with me when I was vulnerable and that is the most amazing gift to give anyone.

TEACHER'S PET

As an empath, unknown to me at my time in school, I was feeling the fear and emotional pain of the other children, occasionally behaving as if it was my event. One such occasion that I remember happened in primary school. At the end of each school year the principal would go from class to class and call the names of those who were moving on to the next year. She would call the names of the children to move on; anyone she didn't call had to remain in their seat while the others stood.

It was a small country school with two classes in each room. Juniors and seniors, first and second, third with fourth and fifth with sixth. When I was in fifth class, the nun started by calling all the names of the sixth-class students and they were led outside to be shown their new school. Then she called the names in fifth class. As each name was called, we stood and took our belongings to the sixth-class area. She called all but one name. One girl was left sitting on her own in the fifth-class area. She sat there and smiled at the nun. But I could feel my heart break, I felt such sadness and injustice. Today I understand that some of this was mine, but I was also putting a copy of the girl's feelings in on top of my own. That day I left my newly designated seat and walked

88

back over and sat beside the 'reject'. The nun laughed at me and walked out of the classroom to transfer up all of the other classes. While she was gone no one spoke as they knew they would have to witness the beating I was likely to receive.

By sixth class, aged eleven, I had accepted that in this life we have to follow rules and conform to society's idea of who we should be. This had now expanded to the realisation that our family background, even our address, influenced our place in society. We were told repeatedly all that we could achieve, or depending on who we were, we were told that we would *"never amount to much."* It seemed that some children could do no wrong, while those of us from small farm holdings or town council estates were judged more harshly.

Occasionally our nun would ask for a volunteer to do a message for her. This could involve going up town to the shop to get milk for her tea, or to bring a message to the Mother House. Even though I always put my hand up I was never chosen. It was always the same few girls that got to escape the classroom. By now I had worked out the meaning of the tenth commandment: "Thou shall not covet thy neighbour's goods." We should not be jealous of what someone else had. If this extended to the preferential treatment some children got over others then yes, I was definitely guilty.

Even at the age of eleven it seemed obvious that unless everyone was treated equally it would cause division. The friends we chose at this young age were those who were treated similarly to ourselves as these were the people we had most in common with. The children the teacher had singled out for preferential treatment, even the way she spoke to them, caused segregation in the classroom and playground. These children had never wronged me, and each were pleasant individuals in their own right, yet there was a difference, not because of anything they had done but because of the views of the nun, her behaviour and her limited beliefs.

One morning is etched in my memory. saw the 'teacher's pet' arrived late. She went up to the nun and whispered to her. This in itself amazed me as I would never have chosen to be in such close proximity to my oppressor. The nun asked for two volunteers. I immediately put up my hand as did all the other children. For this one and only time, smiling, the nun chose me and a child from a council estate. We should have known this was not good. The girl had been sick on the stairwell and we were to clean it up!

When society segregates based on religion, class, culture, or ethnicity they harm both the group receiving the preferential treatment and those receiving inferior treatment. As adults we can now reassess our views of different groups and release some prejudicial judgements which may have been indoctrinated into us by those tasked with our care and education.

The classroom is not the only place where we may have experienced different treatment. This can also be the case in our homes. So many of the clients I meet carry emotional scars from the treatment they received from their parents compared to the way their siblings were treated. This can also be the case in single-child families if a child is led to believe that they are the most special child that ever existed. Eventually this belief will be challenged. Or sometimes an only child can be made to feel insufficient, that they are not enough, that their parents wanted more children and have to settle for this one child.

It is wonderful to love and encourage our children, to teach them that there is no one any better than them. It is equally important that they are no better than anyone else. Encouraging a child to believe they deserve the best and their needs should always come first is setting them up for a fall. When they enter school, college or careers, they will still be judged but this time not on their address, their parents' occupation or income, they will be judged by their character, their work and contribution.

There are many amazing people who do so much for their communities, often going unnoticed - feeding the hungry, offering a comforting ear, fund raising and visiting the sick. Similarly, to how we are treated by our parents and teachers when we were little, those who choose to volunteer at community level, all have the opportunity to add to, or reduce the emotional baggage of those in their care.

In recent years I have had lots of interactions with teachers and special needs assistants. I have been deeply touched by their concern and ingenuity. I have watched them work to find ways to bring out the best in each child, while still teaching the children to comply with the rules.

I have been pleasantly surprised by the number of teachers that are also empaths. Some are so sensitive that they can even pick up on the stress of their students from their homework and exam papers. Each one will have their own challenges, but the sooner they have the realisation that the emotions they often feel are in fact those of the students in their care, or of their fellow work colleagues and not their own, their lives will be so much easier.

The following is a testimonial of a teacher from a pre-school in South Africa, who struggled to let go her emotional connections with her little students.

DOWNLOAD

MAJ

SESSION I

I first met Bríd when I arrived in Ireland in April 2017. I had finally come to a decision to pack my home, leave my pre-school and move to Ireland and answer a deep void within myself. To consciously create a peaceful life with love around me, and a space to be...sea, sky, green, open-ended possibilities. My sister has lived in Ireland for the past twelve years and so I came to her home.

When I arrived, I was very emotional, tired and felt sick. I had packed on 16kg of weight and felt pretty yucky. I longed for a dream of a 'download' I had glimpsed in a meditation, and it had left me with a quiet knowing. My sister had brought me to Bríd on the second day after my arrival. Bríd blessed me and I felt a cocoon of love and light around me. I felt secure. I felt a peace, simple and uncomplicated.

Bríd linked me to her friend, who met me a few days later and took me to the sea and I slowly realised that Bríd must have seen my 'download' and I saw the spaces that had filled me with the deep longing to come to Ireland.

Ireland opened to me and I started to see the beauty and felt the feelings of age and timelessness. The neighbour singing every morning, filled me with love and I just wanted to hug her and tell her that she sings for us all and not to stop. A part of me long, long, forgotten began to wake up, I felt a lot better.

SESSION II

I was privileged to have a second session with Bríd a month later. I was battling with myself. I was not as young as I felt and I had left behind me my *'boootiful'* school which I loved. A feeling of guilt and concern as to whether I had made the correct decision held me back. I had a sore knee, sore back, stiff neck, and was very emotional.

I ached with the pain of indecision. I had a deep 'download' to move on, to lead a simpler life, to embrace my next stage of being sixty – ish +++. Bríd listened to me, heard me, felt my ache and began.

She asked me to close my eyes and guided me to my favourite church and it popped into my head. The church in Johannesburg. A place I had been so comfortable in my early days of nursing. She then asked me to invite each and every child I had loved, cherished and taught at my pre-school of thirty-three years to join me and take them to the alter.

Bríd sat next to me and 'saw' what I saw. She narrated my inner vision as my 'boootiful' children came forth and presented themselves. She described them and I knew them, their names, their faces, and visualised their warm trusting hands in my hand. Tears poured down my cheeks. I ached and chocked with love and emotion. She helped me to cut the cords, with the aid of Arch Angel Michael, with great peace and love. I felt their energy and their open unconditional trust and being. I blessed them all and hugged them.

I found our blessed happy school sing in me and what felt like five minutes was in fact more than an hour-long session. Bríd suggested that I stop looking back at what was, stop being guilty for wanting to move on and let go my fear to jump into a new beginning.

She asked me to listen to my Inner voice that was pulling me to make the change, start new, to be and begin a new stage of an already blessed and privileged life.

I am filled with an inner excitement of what is, what can be and the daily path of new faces, feelings, people, ways and an overwhelming feeling I can be anything, create anything I want.

Thank you Bríd, I will take it step by step, not get caught in past, only draw the good that is and take forth …. Bless you 'boootiful' lady.

LOVE?

At the age of twelve, with my emotional suitcases packed to breaking point, I joined the teenagers in secondary school. I was expected to be ready to be a young adult and learn some new rules.

Similar to the nun who believed 'lefties' were in league with the devil, we each have our own beliefs that we have brought from our childhood and our life experiences. From the moment we arrived on this planet, we are able to work out whether we are hungry or not; if we are in pain, if we are hot or cold, whether it is light or dark. Pretty much everything else has been programmed by family, carers, teachers, peers, literature and media.

I have slowly come to realise that the nun was doing her best with her beliefs. She had no understanding of special needs or of people with empathic ability. She really thought that if we were not able to do the task in hand, she could somehow beat it into us and was therefore helping us to learn and have a better chance in the world.

Some eastern religions actively teach their children to be able to accept compliments as well as material goods. By doing this they believe it will help their children learn and progress in life. They believe the children who are able to accept compliments do better in life than those who, for some reason, have an inability to accept praise. They have a saying that *"When one is unable to accept, one is like an overturned vase, which cannot hold any sweet dew from heaven."*

This is the opposite to how many children are reared. Many of us would be familiar with the criticism of being vain if we stopped to look in the mirror. We struggle to accept a compliment believing that it is somehow wrong or vain. We are told that vanity is one of the seven deadly sins. (I never asked what the other six were. I thought it was safer not to draw attention to any of my other crimes.) We list all the things we see wrong with our image rather than seeing the beauty therein. When our clothing is complimented, many of us answer with a personal put down like *"This old thing," "I got it on sale"* or *"It hides a multitude."* When we go into our adult relationships, if we are unable to see our own value and accept a compliment, without a need for personal criticism, it does not bode well.

When I received the following testimonial, I struggled with it, and with the compliments it contained. I thought *"How am I going to include this?"* Then I thought that if I tell my clients to accept compliments, I also need to learn to do the same thing.

THE GUARDIAN
MARY MCGUANE

Bríd's kind and gentle presence is the guiding signature of all her interactions. She has at her command a range of tools and techniques and engages these with skilful insight to tease out and untangle the webs and layers of presenting concerns and situations. Bríd's pervasive empathy and supportive companionship journeys with clients to the core resonance of the issue. She imparts knowledge and communicates concepts with incisive clarity, generously sharing the wisdom that she effortlessly carries. She is a true and authentic guardian of the wisdom lineage.

As young adults we hurry to find relationships so that we can be the same as our peers. We can't be the only one without a date for our debs, or the only one who hasn't *'done it'!* In our eagerness to be the same we don't necessarily choose our first mate wisely. It can be a matter of who asks us out, or who accepts our invitation, rather than who we are most attracted to, who we have most in common with, or even whose company we enjoy. We also know that in life we will be judged by our peers on our mate's appearance, academic success, popularity, job, income, property and material success. It would appear that society partly judges our personal success by the credentials of our chosen partner.

Add to this list the emotional baggage that we have been collecting throughout our childhood. What kind of relationship do we believe we deserve? For my debs I finally got up the courage to ask my older brother's friend to be my date. I practiced the sentences until I was finally brave enough to ask him. His answer was just one word "No." My confidence took such a hammering. If this was any ordinary function it would be bad enough but this was my debs and I had no date.

Two of my friends were dating teenagers from the next town. A friend of theirs had not been asked but wanted to go for the craic. He agreed to be my date. He sat with me for the meal and I didn't see him for the rest of the night. Despite my sadness that I didn't really have a boyfriend and was only pretending, I knew that at least for the photos and the meal I had succeeded in doing what was expected of me. I had a date for my debs!

Three years later I was employed, as a secretary, in London for a small stock broking firm. They were not aware of my struggles with spelling as I hadn't mentioned that at the interview! This was when typing was done by typewriter and not with computers that highlighted and corrected spelling mistakes.

On my second day at the company the accountant was really struggling to balance the monthly accounts. I offered to look at it. I had done basic bookkeeping in school, not to any higher level, but had always loved it. In desperation he gave me the accounts to look at. Within a few minutes I spotted his error. He had omitted to carry over an entry. I pointed this out to him. He went into the manager's office. On returning he informed me I was now working as a settlement's supervisor. I didn't know what that was, but I knew it meant working with numbers instead of letters. I absolutely loved my new world of phones constantly ringing and a room full of computer listings, which tracked changing stock prices and lots of calculations. Looking back, I think I was partly feeling the heightened awareness of the brokers, many of whom seemed to live on coffee and cigarettes, as well as my own happiness.

One day the accountant asked me to go to Threadneedle Street, the banking area in London, in relation to a bond transaction. I had never been to that area of London before and was still new to the world of bonds. While waiting in the underground for a connecting train I saw a young man staring at me. I had by now adjusted to city life, where we avoid eye contact with all strangers, which was the complete opposite of how I was raised. Growing up we had learnt to acknowledge everyone we met. I felt uncomfortable and silently prayed that if he wanted help with directions, he would ask someone else. But no, this handsome young man kept staring over and finally approached me. *"Hello"* he said. *"Hi"* *"Don't you recognise me?"* he asked. *"No, sorry"* I replied still hoping this stranger would walk away and leave me alone. *"I was your date for your debs!"* *"Oh."*

We chatted awkwardly for a few minutes. He named a number of people from his hometown, who I would be vaguely familiar with, who were now living in London. He asked if I would like to meet up with their group sometime. Being so preoccupied with the task in hand, I politely and quickly excused myself and went about my business. This encounter had always bothered me as I could not understand my reaction or more accurately my lack of reaction. It is only now with an understanding of my empathic ability that I can completely understand it.

On other occasions, when I have been asked out or had similar interactions with the opposite sex, I have unknowingly picked up on their energy and felt some of their feelings. This has influenced my behaviour. Sometimes I agreed to meet up for a drink and later on realised I had nothing in common with this individual and couldn't understand why I had said yes and was then faced with the embarrassing task of talking myself out of any further meeting.

Whereas on that day in the underground I was completely in my own energy. I was solely focused on the task in hand and completely in my own power. At no stage during our brief encounter did I feel any of his emotions. I have no idea what he was feeling, whether he was attracted to me, whether now more mature he regretted his behaviour at my debs or was he just being friendly and thinking it would be good to include me in his group of friends? I have learnt so much from this brief interaction. I learnt that when I am solid in my own energy, I am much less likely to be influenced by the energy of others. In these moments, if I do pick up on something outside of myself, I will notice it much quicker and be able to call in assistance and disconnect.

CREATING OUR REALITY

As we grow up, we are programmed to believe many of our parents and teachers' beliefs and carry these into our adult lives. One Irish saying you may be familiar with is *"money doesn't grow on trees"* and of course it doesn't. On hearing this reply in answer to some of my teenage requests for new trainers, or the latest item of clothing that everyone else seemed to have, I took this saying to imply that I shouldn't ask for anything unnecessary. I brought this belief with me into my adult life. Some new things I could justify, new clothes and shoes for work, but if it was just something that I liked but couldn't justify, I often didn't buy it.

Sometimes an expression can have very different meanings to different people. *"There is no place like home"* can for some of us bring a loving, safe feeling, while for others it can instil fear. It can imply that when we leave home, we won't be safe or able to adapt, or it can imply that we should be grateful for what we have and not look for more. Depending on the tone used and the context, it can imply that we are ungrateful and unappreciative for what we have been given.

Similarly, depending how it is said, repeated expressions can encourage or discourage us travelling out into the world. It can be *"a big bad world"* or a *"wonderful world or endless opportunity."* All of us will have taken on beliefs. Growing up in the same family our siblings can have taken different versions or different beliefs. Depending on where we come in the pecking order or what was going on in the lives of our family members, we can have been programmed completely differently to other children that were reared in the same house.

"I have to mind my siblings" or *"I am minded by my siblings."*

"I should put others first" or *"My needs come first."*

"Never say No" or *"People will never say no to me."*

When working as a healer I take on a complete photocopy of my clients' physical and emotional pain. I use this information to identify limiting beliefs that are slowing down their personal growth or negatively impacting on their life. The symbols that form my Psychic Code can be in picture format. I may hear a line from a song or nursery rhyme. It can be a smell, or through my empathic gift I may feel something in my own body.

These are my references with meanings that are my interpretation. People develop their psychic code that is unique to them. The same image can have different interpretation for different people. For example, when I see the image of a rose in my mind's eye this is my symbol for an upcoming anniversary being acknowledged. I look at the stem for the thorns, the more thorns I see, the more difficult the relationship was. A lack of thorns indicates a loving and positive relationship. A psychic image of a rose represents pure love for one of my friends. While for another friend the smell of roses is a sign her grandmother (who grew roses) is with her.

While channelling, any sensation I feel on the right side of my body refers to the person's past while anything to my left refers to the present. For example, if I feel my body tilting to the right, that's my symbol that the person didn't feel they had support in their childhood; that there wasn't anyone standing at their side. They may not have had anyone to share their problems with. They may have had to shoulder more responsibility than society expects of a child. If I tilt to the left it's my reference to present day - that they do not have somebody to help them now. They currently feel unsupported.

I have symbols for addiction, betrayal, fear, physical abuse, sexual abuse, legal issues, co-dependency and many more. Putting the information together I come to an understanding of the person, their personality, their family dynamics, struggles and inherited beliefs. Using this information, we work together to let go their physical and emotional pain.

One woman that came to see me had constant pain in the bones in her neck, to the point where she was considering very risky surgery. She hadn't been in an accident and could find no explanation of where the pain originated from. As I empathically felt a copy of her pain, in my mind's eye I was shown pictures from her childhood. She had found it hard to focus on one task at a time and was always been told off for forgetting things. I could hear her mother scolding her and telling her *"You would forget your head if it wasn't tied on."* Believing her mother, she had started hunching her shoulders and bringing her head down as low as possible to prevent her mother's prediction coming true.

I explained to her the reason she was so forgetful was because she was an empath and was constantly picking up on the energy of others. As a young child and with no understanding of her gift she was unable to focus. We went through the steps for connecting and disconnecting from energy. Then we did some work on her inner child, letting go her beliefs that she was not good enough and was a disappointment to the grown-ups in her life. We assured her inner child that it was safe to walk with her shoulders relaxed and her head held high.

I consider it a privilege to 'walk in other people's shoes' while briefly experience their life and coming to an understanding of what they have been through. In the following story we see a client recognising her struggle with feelings of dejection and lack of confidence and seek out answers to unlock where these issues originated. By trusting in an unseen power her enthusiasm for life was restored along with a newfound belief in herself.

FATE

MARY BURKE

I have been favoured by fate to know Bríd and experience her empathic healing gift on more than one occasion. This healing has provided emotional and physical relief in a manner that couldn't be foreseen. I have known Bríd for some years from a meditation group, which she leads. I decided to attend for a one-to-one healing session, as I had a sense of dejection and felt less than confident in asserting my own needs when involved in groups. I had increasingly felt frustrated (even bullied) in group events.

Bríd sat with me in our healing session and described a little girl she saw in national school. The child was being heavily managed by a teacher - how to draw, how to behave - more than the average discipline required for a child.

I remembered this situation well, and a specific event which took place when I was six years old. The teacher asked me to sell tickets door to door in the town near where we lived. I was really frightened and didn't want to knock on all the doors asking for money. I also knew we couldn't buy all the tickets (at home) ourselves. So, I told the teacher that I couldn't take the tickets to sell them. She was very cross and sent for my mother after school. Such a summons was a major event.

I waited that evening for the outcome of the meeting - on one hand dreading the prospect of going door to door, but on the other hand, dreading the outcome of the parent/teacher meeting. My mother came home and explained that I did not have to sell the tickets. However, she said I had to sincerely apologise to the teacher on the following morning. An ordeal which I didn't relish (as I hadn't done anything wrong) - but the lesser of two evils.

I didn't (at six) know the words powerless or humiliation, but I certainly knew the feeling that went with them. Some resolve must have kicked in at that stage, to avoid humiliation in the future. This translated into losing ability to say what I wanted (and even not knowing myself what I wanted) – anything to avoid humiliation or confrontation with strong minded folks. I'm an intelligent person, but spent many years avoiding humiliation, often showing anger instead at those close to me.

The healing session released that awful sense of oppression and the need to roll in with what the 'strong demanding' others asked. The healing exercise itself was so compassionate, but also a life tonic. The message I took away was also very simple to apply - remember the little girl who finds her voice. When in doubt about where I stand, or asserting my need, I go back to that space and state clearly what I can do/not do. I am reminded that my needs have to be listened to, and this enables me to believe that it was perfectly all right to operate within the boundaries I set. I felt empowered and happier in my interactions with everyone. That healing session freed that vulnerable child and gave the child the ability to believe in her perfectly reasonable and sincere wishes and beliefs. I thank God and Bríd for restoring my enthusiasm for life and belief in myself.

It's wonderful to come to the realisation that as we declutter from some of the negative programming, we can replace it with new positive beliefs that are more suitable to our current journey. It is liberating to know that we can revisit our beliefs and affirmations and change these as we change. As a seven-year-old I had made the decision that I did not want to feel pain anymore. In later years I developed a nerve disorder. I now understand that it is safe to feel pain and that as an adult I am allowed to say "No." The body is very clever and will come up with very specific ways of granting our wishes and beliefs.

Thankfully I now see my psychic abilities as a gift. I have the ability to know when someone is in emotional turmoil even if they are pretending otherwise. I call in whatever help and assistance is appropriate. I know it is in the best interest of all my loved ones, my friends and my clients that I myself am well, safe and provided for. I have learnt to prioritise my own care.

When I am in a good space my work is busy, both with clients and workshops. However, when I have not been taking care of myself, have been overdoing it, over giving, or slipping back into old patterns of never saying "No", my clients literally cancel. Entire days of client bookings can simply cancel their appointments. My guides and the guides of my clients know that if I am exhausted, or not taking care of myself, then there is no point going ahead with the appointments.

One of the new beliefs that I have programmed is that my angels keep my diary. When I look at my diary and see future dates that have no bookings, I know there is a reason that has yet to be revealed. Come that day there will be a family issue, or perhaps local flooding or stormy conditions. My angels always know best.

Every one of us will have our own story, our own perception, our own beliefs. It is wonderful when we are able to find a key and open one of these prison doors.

The author of the following story tells how she did just that.

ICE SKATING
WIESLAWA

My Sister asked me again *"Did you buy the ticket yet? When are you coming over?"*

"Ooo Marysia stop" I said. *"I was with you only a few months ago. I am still recovering. Can you come over to visit me for a change?"* As soon as I said it, I knew it was silly of me to ask that question. Of course, my younger sister could not come to visit me, despite how much she would like to. She is minding our ninety-one-year-old Mum. Not that Mum is unable to mind herself, but she is quite forgetful and fearful and none of us would leave her alone for more than a couple of hours. This fear runs in our family. I am very like my Mum in personality and in appearance.

I still remember sixty-four years ago the fear I felt when I was locked in the house alone and I

114

escaped by climbing out of a broken window at three years of age. It was a hot summer's day at lunchtime. My Mum and I were living at my grandparents' house in the country. Everyone had to work very hard those days. There wasn't time to mind children in the way one would like to. My Mum put me down to have a little nap in her bed and went out to do some work in the nearby field. Most children would have experienced this as a pleasurable event and even when they did wake up earlier than usual, they could stay in bed and wait for someone to come back. I was not very patient then and even less now. When I woke up there was nobody around. I got quite nervous and panicky. I tried to open the heavy wooden front door but it was no use. I was too small to reach the handle. I saw the light shining in the window. Even though it was a small window, for me it was the way out.

I was adventurous even then and the stress levels helped me as well. It didn't take me long to figure out how to get out. There were enamel mugs hanging on the wall near the window. I grabbed the white one, climbed onto the bench, which was by the window and I started to work on the glass window panel. I couldn't care less about the blood pouring out of my arms and my legs, or even my neighbour, who heard the noise of broken glass and came out of her house shouting at me to stop!!!

"Mum will be back in a second. Wait !" But I did not hear her. I did not feel the pain or see the blood pumping out of my body. I was free. Or wait, was I? Not really.

That was the first time I remember feeling fear. Since then, there have been so many times that I have felt this emotion. I did not know or even dream that one day, I could be free of that feeling. I went to primary school. At the age of thirteen I was sent to a boarding school. I stayed there for four years. That experience could make you or break you. It didn't break me, but it did a lot of damage and my fears were starting to have a greater effect on my life.

After university my first job was with the Polish Airlines. The excitement and yes, my friend, the fear, was all the time with me. I got married to an Irish man wo didn't speak a word of Polish. I spoke what was considered in school to be advanced English *"Yes please, No thank you"* and a couple of more words, I could even count up to ten.

Life went on for me. I was now living in a foreign country, with foreign food, foreign climate and with a foreign husband whom I met through writing letters hoping to learn English. But guess what? My one familiar friend stayed with me. My best friend, the fear! We went together through my breakdown, depression, anxiety, losing my marriage, losing my business. She was there all that time, what a friend!

It was only at this point that I decided enough was enough. My Mum, my sister, my niece and my son were all abroad and would love to have seen me and I really, really, wanted to see them. The medication did not work. Every time I bought a plane ticket to travel home, I felt paralysed and I was not able to go on the flight because of fear.

Just a year ago a friend said, *"You have tried everything and nothing works."* "Yep", I said *"That is true."* She asked, *"Will you try something less conventional like visiting a healer?"* "There is nothing to lose" I said.

First, we went to one of Bríd s workshops, just more for curiosity then for anything else. To be honest with you, I really don't remember much of what it was all about but Bríd made a massive impact on me. What a beautiful person and she likes foxgloves! That is my favourite flower. The white ones are the nicest, in Bríd's and my opinion anyway.

After the workshop I arranged an appointment to meet Bríd in her beautiful, peaceful, place which is so full of warmth. She welcomed me into her house. We had a small chat just for a couple minutes. As I was early for my appointment, she left me for five minutes or so. When she came back in, I felt very relaxed and we started the session. I felt very relaxed throughout the appointment. I did not say much to her about my problems with fear beforehand. As the time went on, I felt more and more relaxed.

With her guidance I travelled back through my memories to a time when I was a young girl. I could picture myself standing nearby an ice-skating lake. I could see other children ice-skating and having a really good time. I was standing all alone on the side of that frozen lake, looking at them with envy, while frozen with fear and not able to join them. I was standing there for a good while in temperatures of minus 25 degrees Celsius.

It wasn't the first time this had happened. I went there every day hoping that one day one of the girls would take me by my hand and bring me with her to skate. Nobody did. I got frost bite on my feet and on my hands from standing there waiting. Suddenly as I watched the memories, I heard Bríd's soft voice saying, *"Go and take this little girl, Wieslawa, by the hand and go skating with her"* and I did. I actually picked her up and we started skating together. The music was playing and we were laughing and dancing. We were wearing beautiful gowns just like on an international ice-skating show.

The little me was so, so, happy and the adult me was holding her so tight telling her how wonderful she was and how much she is loved. I really did not want to stop the music and the dancing it was so enjoyable and so special and loving for me and this little girl.

Bríd then calmly and gently told me what had happened during my session within me. She repeated the journey I had visualised and it was exactly what I had experienced. The peace I felt afterwards was something I will never forget.

For a week or so I felt like I was in 'cloud cuckoo-land'. I went around smiling to myself and felt happy out. I wasn't sure exactly what had happened during my session with Bríd and wondered if it would work.

Bríd did tell me as the session ended that I had connected with my childhood and the events that had happened at the ice-skating lake very well. She believed that my fear shouldn't be such a burden to me in the future.

"Okay wonderful" I said to myself. I was dying to prove to myself that it really had worked. The next day I bought myself a ticket to Poland and was waiting for my body's reaction which usually accompanied me throughout my years of flying anywhere any time; anxiety, panic attacks, diarrhoea, vomiting etc. Guess what? That never happened again.

A few months after I came back from Poland, I went to see my son in America for the first time since he had gone to live there nine years earlier. I have my life back.

Thank you Bríd for being the channel between the Maker of me and the fearful child of sixty-four years ago.

Blessing to you and yours.

Love Wieslawa

WHO AM I?

Different people will be more impacted by different emotions. The environment we grew up in contributes to how we are affected. If we grew up in a home with someone suffering from depression, we are more likely to be impacted by this emotion when we encounter it in others. Likewise, if we grew up where there was constant fear, then fear is the feeling we will quickly pick up on from others.

Those with empathic ability who had a parent with constant anxiety are likely to merge into the energy of those they meet in their everyday life who suffer from anxiety. Where a parent is struggling to complete any task, unable to concentrate or moving from one idea to another without completing anything, their empathic child may find themselves struggling to concentrate when in similar company. Even if the empathic child may normally be someone who is very calm, steady and productive they will be affected by their parent's energy. This is the energy we are familiar with. We recognise this energy; we have lived it in our childhood. If we take on a copy of it from our new friend, partner or work colleague we are used to wearing this sweater.

No matter how badly the adult tasked with our care treats us, we still desperately want their love and approval. We want them to notice us. We want them to like us. They are the leader of our pack and we want them to be proud of us. This does not just apply to our home environment, it can also be in the classroom, youth club, sports club, social group, etc. As adults we can carry this need into our relationships and workplace. Different people will adopt different tactics.

The **Rebel** will be defiant. They will do what has to be done, but their oppressor will be in no doubt that they are not happy with the situation. They may organise walk outs and they may shout from the roof tops about the treatment they and their colleagues are receiving. Sometimes, however, they may be so stuck in their moment of injustice that the pleasant and joyful moments pass them by unnoticed. Some rebels act behind closed doors, complaining about others when they are out of earshot.

The empath who takes on a copy of the rebel can find themselves in the firing line and wonder how they got there. One lady I was speaking with recently explained how she attends weekly meetings at work. Every week she promises herself that she is not going to say anything negative. She likes her job and generally is happy with the way the company is run. However, when she attends these meetings, she ends up getting really worked up and comes across as being hostile.

She was so relieved to come to a better understanding of her empathic ability. I asked her which staff member was always going to war and always unhappy with work conditions. Immediately she understood what had been happening. I suggested that before attending any further meetings she stops for a moment to take a few deep breaths, ground herself and ask her angels to help her remain strong in her own energy. In future, when she feels the urge to speak at the meeting, I asked her to again disconnect and sit with it for a moment to see if this was something she felt strongly about or if it was in fact the energy of her colleague that she was acting on.

The **Victim** can only see the impact of the negative treatment on their own life. They can enter into a dark space where there is fear, pain and sorrow. This is a truly difficult place to return from, to reconnect with the joy and love the world has to offer. Some will make every effort to crawl their way out of that dark space, while others will believe there is no return.

When in a copy of this energy, we can miss out on all the things that usually bring us joy as our focus now goes to the negative. We can step out of our own normal energy and replace it with a copy of the fear, pain and sorrow being experienced by the other individual. Once we enter this space, we no longer participate in life the way we would normally do. Our relationships with our family, friends and work colleagues are impacted.

The **Class Clown** has given up trying to please the parent, teacher or manager. Instead, the clown decides to make themselves the centre of attention for their social group's approval. They have decided to get other children's notice and friendship by appearing not to take life seriously, but all the time they crave attention and approval.

The **Helper** will do whatever they can to improve the lot of others, irrespective of the consequences for themselves. When I was in sixth-class, we had weekly spelling and maths tests. Our nun would write the correct answers on the board and we swapped our copy books with another child to correct them. One week I got my spelling book back with 8/10. This was an amazingly high score for me, - too amazing! So much so that the nun came to check the result and realised the child who was tasked with my corrections had in fact marked incorrect spellings as being correct. She was slapped for her efforts to help me. To this day I am still grateful to her. As an empath I had felt her sense of injustice on my behalf, her fear and her pain as well as my gratitude and guilt.

There is the **Invisible Observer**. If it were possible, they would melt into the wall. When we look back at our school photos there will be the child whose name we struggle to remember. They opt to live life unnoticed as much as possible. This is a big price to pay for survival. I occasionally took on this survival method in my childhood. I found it so much easier to be on the verge of the group observing rather than participating. It felt safer, though I did not fully understand why.

Many empaths are constantly bombarded by the energy of others, but we do not understand what is happening. We know that we leave home with one set of feelings but as soon as we meet someone, we can literally change personality. The pain we collect can be overwhelming. One way to survive is to become the invisible observer and shut down our hearts so we feel nothing. By doing so we are making a conscious decision to keep our emotional participation in life to the minimum.

The **Peacemaker** is always coming up with solutions. Sometimes in their efforts to keep the peace they may prevent others from standing up for themselves. If this peacemaker stands between the bully and the victim on a regular basis, they can prevent the victim from finding their own voice and standing up for themselves. The peacemaker may go on to be the victim's hero. But unknowingly and unintentionally they may be doing the victim a huge disservice. When the victim leaves school and goes into the adult world of relationships and work environments they do so never having learnt to say no and without being confident to stand up for themselves. They have learnt to stand behind the peacemaker.

The **Perfectionist** will stay at their homework until every aspect is perfect. This, they believe will win them approval or set themselves at a high standard. They may always feel under stress and pressure as they strive for perfection. As the perfectionist child grows, the physical and emotional toll mounts with the increased tasks and homework. Finally, their body reaches breaking point or maybe someday they are forced to stop and re-evaluate.

Both the perfectionist, and any empath who is in the copy of their energy, are often under huge stress. The pressure on their chest can feel physical. In this energy the perfectionist does tasks based on what they perceive is expected by others and by their own extreme standards.

I compare this to cleaning windows. When I clean my own windows, I get a bucket of soapy water, wash with one cloth and polish with a dry cloth. Without fuss or anxiety, I get the job done, often singing as I work.

If I go into perfectionist mode, I start overanalysing, asking myself *"How do others do this? What is the correct way to proceed? Should I polish with newspapers?"* I don't use newspapers myself when doing this job so if I now try to do this I will be stressed as it's going to streak. Or maybe I should use a power washer! I have rarely used a power washer and when I have done so I have always had help. Now, in the energy of the perfectionist, I'd be wondering how far back to stand, how much detergent and how much pressure. Whereas if I did it my normal way, the windows will be cleaned to a good enough standard that I am happy with. When we get into the perfectionist mode, wanting the approval of others, we live in constant stress. Rather than working comfortably to our strengths we try to do things the way we perceive others would expect them done.

One client who came to meet me lived a life of constant stress. I could feel the weight on her chest to the point where her breathing was laboured. In my mind's eye I could see her as a seven-year-old child standing in her kitchen facing the wall. I asked the client what this memory represented. She explained that her sister, who was ten years older than her, was usually tasked with her care and also with checking her homework. This sister was her mother's 'right-hand-man' and could do no wrong. Whatever she said seemed to become law.

This older sister wanted to be a teacher. Any time the client got her homework wrong or had not completed the tasks to her sister's standard, she had to stand facing the wall until her sister decided to let her turn around. This happened when other family members were present and even if they had visitors. She went on to live a life of constant stress, fearing if she got anything wrong it would be found out and she would be publicly reprimanded. We worked together to take the weight off the seven-year-old, to tell her that she was good enough and she is loved.

The **Pleaser** will do everything in their power to make the parent, teacher or employer like them. This character will rarely voice their own opinion; they will accept without complaint the work load they are given.

The pleasers can go on to be adults that always put the needs of others first. Until they reach breaking point or finally realise that their needs and views have equal importance. I think there may be a bit of the pleaser in all of us.

Then add into the mix our own unique and complex personality. We are each a completely unique combination of our parents' DNA, our grandparents' DNA and DNA inherited from previous generations. Add to this mix our own childhood experiences and beliefs, our nature and the level of nurturing we have received. In addition to this, the empath child is bombarded with the feelings of others. Generally, they have no awareness or understanding of this ability and receive no explanation or advice as they go out into the world to try and navigate their way.

At my workshops, many empaths express that they do not have a clear picture of who they are when they are in their own energy. They don't know how to make individual decisions, as they always go with what the other person is feeling. They are concerned that when they step into their own energy, they may just find a void. Often empaths can blend into the emotions of others to the point where they themselves almost disappear.

I have come to realise that I have much more to contribute to friendships when I am being my true self. If I remain strong in my own energy, instead of being emotionally unpredictable or drained I get to be myself; I answer as me. I am of more use, more logical and more able to do good when I am fully myself. The more time I spend living in my energy the better I get to know myself. Writing my books and facilitating meditations and workshops has been of great benefit to me. It has helped me to understand my past, heal from it and become comfortable in my own skin.

GEOPATHIC STRESS

Many of us are aware of different types of energy. Apart from picking up on the energy of our loved ones and those we interact with in our daily routine, many are also impacted by:

1. **Geopathic energy**

2. **Residual energy**

3. **Soul energy**

We may not understand on a conscious level why we don't want to go into a building or sit on a specific chair. Maybe we feel tired when visiting a certain location. Perhaps we know something negative has happened in a building even though we have not been told this. We may be picking up on energy other than the emotions of the people we come into contact with.

The level to which we are affected by different types of energy will depend on our personal level of sensitivity. The more sensitive you are, the greater the impact your environment will have on you. Therefore, the need for and the amount of effort you put into energy clearing will vary, depending on how affected you are. Compare someone who is a minimalist in their home versus someone who is a collector or hoarder. When it comes to giving our home a spring clean, the minimalist will get through their house cleaning much faster. There is a lot less to clean. Shelves can be quickly wiped down, corners can be accessed, cobwebs are visible. The collector, on the other hand, will have to wash or dust each ornament, each piece of crystal, each item will need to be washed and dried individually, cabinets holding the many items may have to be moved to clean behind them. The more possessions we own, the more cleaning required. Similarly, the more sensitive we are to energy, the more we will have to work on clearing it.

Of the above list, geopathic energy is probably the easiest one to explain. There is scientific evidence to back up this theory.

The planet Earth has its own magnetic energy field. This differs from the magnetic field on other planets. Our bodies, and indeed everything that lives on our planet, have developed over time to enable us to live in this particular energy field. Continuous signals from our brain control our body and enable us to function in this atmosphere. Sometimes however, there can be interference to the magnetic field.

If for example, there is a narrow stream of water below ground, even a considerable distance underground, this can create its own electromagnetic field. As the Earth's natural vibration passes through the electromagnetic field in the stream it is capable of distorting the Earth's natural resonance in that area. Likewise, if a property is built over certain mineral concentrations, fault lines or underground cave systems, they can similarly impact on the Earth's natural vibration. Many people believe that the vibration can be impacted in a similar way by some man-made constructions for example, underground railways, electric pylons and masts.

Concentrated geopathic energy can blot out the signals to our brain in such a way that the natural flow of information to the cells, glands and organs is interrupted or even stopped. This can have an adverse effect on our bodies. The stronger the disturbance, the weaker the flow of information in our bodies and the more noticeable the symptoms become. I believe that the more sensitive a person is, the more they will be affected by this disruption.

These are some of the indicators to look out for if you think there could be geopathic energy negatively affecting your home.

Is there a specific area in the building where you always feel exhausted?

Do you never feel refreshed after a night's sleep.

Is someone in the house prone to fluid-based illness, such as kidney infections, and are these symptoms not as noticeable if spending time elsewhere?

Is your lymph system not working properly and are you retaining fluid without an alternative cause?

Do you seem to have more energy when you are outside of your home?

Are you living on a fault line?

Is there a problem with runoff water that is collecting near or under your home?

Is there poor drainage at the property?

If you think there may be an issue in your home or work-space you can try out some simple things before deciding on a definite cause, or before spending lots of money rectifying a problem you may not have.

You could move the chair or bed slightly.

Try sleeping in a different room.

Add some copper off cuts, or a copper ornament in that area and see if it makes a positive difference.

If you are able to douse with a rod or pendulum, you could use this to check if there is a problem and to identify where the line is running. This is the same technique used when divining for water. Growing up I watched diviners using a metal clothes hanger or a branch of a willow tree when trying to locate an underground spring. In the past, many homes in rural areas had their own supply of water before water schemes were provided. Every area had people that were known to be able to divine for water.

If the symptoms persist, there are steps you can take to counteract them. Many people work specifically with geopathic energy fields and there are lots of websites and books on the topic. There are numerous items you can purchase that may help, for example, neutraliser rods, neutraliser pyramids, radiation protector pyramids, orgone pyramids and copper pyramids. Many crystals are believed to have properties that assist with minimising the impact of the stress. I suggest that you do some research before purchasing any of these.

While growing up in rural Ireland there was no shortage of folklore and ghost stories. Different townlands had paranormal events that were unique to that area. These happenings were often experienced before a death in that community. Some were unique to a particular family, and when people moved to other townlands the supernatural events continued to occur in their new homes. For some it would present as a knock to the door. When the door was answered there would be no one there but within twenty-four hours there would be a death in the family. Sometimes the clock would stop at a certain time for no apparent reason, but later the household would learn of a relative passing at that time.

For some the news would come in their dreams. Other families, my paternal grandmother included, would hear or see the banshee. In certain areas a ball of light would pass through the home. Some graveyards would have a ball of light appear at night-time in the week before someone would be buried there. A bird coming into the home can be a warning of an imminent death. These are more than customs. It is a connection; a communication and a message of preparation being passed from an invisible source. It wasn't questioned, it was accepted as part of life.

As we grew and played further from home the rules did not just include the usual, *"Don't talk to strangers" "Have manners"* but we also knew never to disrespect a fairy fort and never take anything from one, not even a stone. We heard many times of the backlash visited on farmers who decided to demolish such forts, how they had serious accidents, that they and future generations were cursed with bad luck and sometimes how the person who had intentionally disrespected the fort died shortly afterwards.

We were also warned about the *Féar Gorta,* the hunger grass. Sometimes, for no apparent reason, when crossing a field one could become completely disoriented and experience hunger pangs. The disorientation would be so overwhelming that it would become impossible to work out how to get out of the field. Or if somehow you did manage to get out, you would be so confused and hungry that you could not find your way home. My father warned us of this and explained what we were to do if we had the misfortune to enter such a place. The instructions were to make your way to any wall in the field. Take off your jacket, or sweater, turn it inside out and put it back on. Then take it off again and turn it back the right way and put it on again. At the end of this process, you should be clear in your thoughts and able to continue your journey.

As a child I thought this must be the work of the *wee folk* but now I wonder if it was geopathic energy from underground water. Depending on the amount of rainfall the affect would vary. Therefore, a field that you had been in many times before and had no such affect could suddenly leave you feeling completely drained and exhausted. The more sensitive you are, the greater the affect. The *'gorta'* was possibly residual energy from the famine. In the Irish language the word Gorta is used both to describe hunger and it is also the word for famine. The advice on how to undo the affect is similar to any energy clearance: you focus your mind on a task, believing that you have the power to change the effect, feeling empowered and trusting it will be all right.

RESIDUAL ENERGY

While out for a walk recently I found myself staggering on the road, struggling to walk in a straight line. As I came around the corner, I saw an empty beer can dumped on the roadside. Immediately I was able to identify what was going on. Someone drunk had recently walked home on the road. The copy of their energy had soaked into the ground. In this instance I did not ask for prayers for the person. They had probably slept off the affects of the alcohol by now. The road was holding a copy of their energy and this is what I was picking up on. The road did not need prayers. Instead, I asked for light to be put down over the area. To release the residual energy and replace it with light.

During a workshop I was running in Dublin a young woman asked for help to understand what was going on in her home. She explained she shared the house with friends who, like her, had all immigrated to Ireland. There was one room in this house, a box room, that never felt nice. She said it made no sense to her as all that was stored in the room was their suitcases. She had made a number of attempts to clear the energy. Smudging the room with sage hadn't made a difference. She had even left the light on in there, but still anytime she had to go into the room she felt like crying even though she was very happy with her new life.

The explanation I was given by my guide, that I repeated to the group, was very interesting. I asked her to recall buying the luggage, how sad she was at having to leave home, how sad her family was every time they had seen her packing. Her sadness at how little she could take with her. Her sadness at all she had left behind. I asked her to recall how heavy her bag had felt as she dragged it to the airport. As she held that suitcase how emotional was her farewell to her parents? This sadness was replicated by each of her friends with their luggage.

I explained that this was the sadness she was feeling every time she entered their box room. This was the energy she needed to name and ask to be released when she was smudging that room or state her intention when leaving on the light. If we are not aware of where the feeling comes from, we can keep it simple, by saying *"Letting out the heaviness/sadness/pain – bringing in the light."* Again, in this instance we are clearing residual energy, the suitcases did not need our prayers, nor did its owners, but the energy attached to them did need clearing.

Land, buildings, possessions, even jewellery can hold residual energy. This is something we feel when we walk into a room. Similar to our empathic ability when picking up on the energy of another individual, we can feel both the physical and emotional symptoms of the energy left behind.

Those of us who are sensitive to residual energy, may consider energy clearing our homes from time to time. Before taking on a task like this it is important that we ourselves are in a good emotional space. If we are having a bad day or just had an argument with a family member, it is not the time for raising the vibration in our home. If we are going around asking for light to be brought in, while in our minds we want to shout at someone, it is not going to work. However, if you wait for the dust to settle, it can be part of the process of taking back your power. Letting go all the pain and hurt and bringing in self-love and self-belief. This can be incredibly liberating.

The steps I use for energy clearing are:

Step 1. Identify the blockages.

Step 2. Choose the wording.

Step 3. Clear the residual energy.

Step 4. Seal the space.

Step 5. Gratitude.

The first thing to note with this is that you cannot do it wrong. It's similar to saying a prayer, you can't say a wrong prayer. When I was aged eleven, a priest came to our classroom to examine us and decide if we were ready for confirmation. We were all asked questions in turn. I was asked what prayer did I say after I receive communion. I recited a little prayer I had been thought at home. *"Jesus is here, sweet Jesus I love you...."* I was quickly told this was the wrong answer and he asked another child the same question. Their prayer was apparently better than mine. Even at the age of eleven I knew that I was not the one who was wrong in this instance. I knew in my heart that there is no wrong prayer once it comes from a place of love. When doing a house clearance, we can't get it wrong but we may discover techniques that we prefer or that seem to have a bigger impact.

Step 1. Identify the blockages.

Work out the places that do not feel pleasant. You might intuitively not like a room or a piece of furniture. You might feel different whenever you are in that space or sitting on a certain chair. Perhaps you don't have a feeling to back up your beliefs, but you may just know that it is not the same as other rooms. As you go through this process you might have recollections of arguments or difficult events like a sick or dying relative, who spent time in that space. As you identify areas that do not feel nice it does not mean something evil has happened here. It can simply be a bedroom where someone has repeatedly cried themselves to sleep. The room is not evil, the energy that does not feel nice is simply a recollection of sadness, fear or loneliness which is being held in this space. It is important to note that it is the negative emotions that are being released. Love and joy can never be deleted.

Residual energy can be found in objects, especially those that are used regularly. If every time we look into the fridge, we think of the lack of food that it contains, then that is the energy that is being built up in that area. The ironing board can get kicked and sworn at. The garden can be seen as a chore instead of a beautiful space to enjoy nature and freedom.

When doing house clearances, I start at the front door and walk around each room, working in a clockwise direction until ending up back where I started. As I do this, I will feel residual energy. Hallways often have heaviness behind the letterbox as people stress over what bills are awaiting them. Sometimes there may be feelings of financial insecurity. However, in more recent years this stress has moved with our paperless billing onto our phones and laptops.

Hallways can hold the memory of the pressure experienced by parents as they return to their homes to 'face in' to mealtime, homework time, and their children's schedule of extra activities, (Johnny football at 7, Maeve, swimming 7.30, collect Johnny at 8 and get back in time for Maeve at 8.30). Alarm systems can often cause more stress than they are supposed to alleviate.

Sitting rooms can be places where arguments occur between couples, arguments between family members over tv programmes, hours spent on computer games killing the bad guy (*"die, die, die"*). For single people, or those in loveless relationships, couches can hold memories of loneliness.

Kitchens can be a stressful place at meal preparation time. I often find memories of tears at kitchen sinks as mums are overwhelmed by what their lives have become. Homework time can leave its own mark. People tend to sit on the same chairs resulting in a build-up of their energy. I can identify who has backache, or various health conditions from the energy left on their chairs. Often there is a build-up of negative emotion around where correspondence is piled or filed.

Bathrooms present their own issues. Baths, showers and lavatories are where we finally relax and let go our stress. The area around mirrors and bathroom scales can hold memories of self-loathing, low confidence or self-criticism.

Bedrooms can repeat many of the above behaviours and emotions. They can hold memories of sadness, loneliness or arguments as well as love, joy and relaxation. If there is a computer game station in our children's bedrooms we can find *"die, die, die,"* vented for hours at a screen. Wardrobes can be another area of self-criticism, self-loathing, possibly feelings of lack as we hold on to clothing that no longer fits us or that we do not even like but feel we should keep, just in case! For those of us who are very sensitive, our clothing can hold memories of difficult events that happened while we were wearing them.

On energy clearing the room of a female client I was very drawn to one of her winter jackets hanging in her wardrobe. On picking it up I felt anxious and panicky. I asked the woman about the jacket. She explained she rarely wears it but recently she had answered a phone call from her sister saying she had fallen and asking that she collect her and bring her to the hospital. She had picked that particular jacket to wear as even though it was summertime, she had felt its warmth comforting. I explained the jacket had absorbed a copy of her energy from that night.

When artists are painting, they can let their guard down and put their energy into every brush stroke of their work. On purchasing one of these paintings, we may feel how the artist felt as they worked on this piece of art. Musicians can be similar to artists in that their energy is very evident in their instruments. When people are reading, they can leave their energy field completely open as they become enthralled in the story. If the book is a scary story, a horror story or a science fiction, their fear can soak into the pages. If it is a history book it can hold the anger or indignation of the reader, and so on. For a lot of empaths, places like libraries, museums and second-hand book shops are very challenging places to visit, let alone work in. I used to feel absolutely exhausted when I spent time in any of these buildings.

Step 2. Choose the wording.

Having walked around your room, house, office, garage, land or wherever it is that you identified the negative residual energy, it is time to work out what you want to replace it with. Depending on your level of sensitivity, you will have identified which memories of emotion or pain the property has absorbed and you are now ready to release. There is no wrong way of doing this, but it is best to avoid negative statements in your wording and keep it simple. The idea is to let God, your angels, or whatever higher power you are invoking, know what it is you want their assistance with.

I describe this as being similar to your relationships with your loved ones. If any of your friends have a problem, you know there is something wrong, but if they don't tell you what it is, or what help they require, then short of offering reassurance, it is very difficult to help. Even if you do know what is wrong, without having the conversation with them and a request for help being made, then with respect to their privacy and right to control their own life, we have little choice but to watch on from a distance while wishing them well.

The same applies to prayer and working with energy, we need to specify our request and we need to accept responsibility. That does not mean the process has to be complicated. Your request can be as simple as:

Letting out the dark, bringing in the light.

Letting out heaviness, bringing in joy.

Letting go the pain of the past and replacing it with joy and happiness.

I let go the past and live in the now.

Letting go sadness and tears, replacing it with joy love and laughter.

Letting go poverty thinking, bringing in abundance.

I step from the brokenness of my past into my new and healthy reality.

I let go loneliness and welcome in friendship and love.

I acknowledge the past and move into a healthier reality.

It is important to remember that as we let go, we need to state what we want to bring in, otherwise we are creating a void. Different issue will be identified in different rooms and therefore a different sentence may be required.

Again, starting in the hallway, we might decide on the sentence *"Letting go poverty thinking and bringing in knowledge of abundance," "Letting go stress and bringing in calmness/tranquillity"* or *"Letting go fear bringing in the knowledge that I am safe."*

In the sitting room *"Letting go loneliness and bringing in love," "Letting go aggression and bringing in peace"* may feel like appropriate sentences to use. Continue in this manner as you work your way around the house, identifying each of the blocked emotions and what you would like to replace them with.

Step 3. Clear the residual energy.

With your sentences worked out, it's now time to pick a tool. You can use almost anything. By using a tool, you are reinforcing your belief that what you are doing is a ritual. This is a real process and it will have real results.

When I say pick a tool, I am suggesting something that you are going to rattle or shake as you walk your property for a second time. It can be a sound bowl, a drum, saucepan lids, a wooden spoon with a biscuit tin or simply clap your hands. Alternatively, you could smudge with sage. Some people will play music in the background, others will open windows, some will set up a little alter, others will light a candle. Do whatever you feel is right.

It is best to establish a simple process for your ritual. This will make it easier each time you need to raise the vibration in your home. By making it into a big production you are setting the belief that this is the way it works. Time may not always permit for a big ritual. If you know that there is a room or a book or piece of jewellery that does not feel right, you do not want to set the belief that you have to clear the whole house in order to address one blockage.

With your tool in hand walk around each room (or just the area that needs urgent attention). Rattle, bang, clap your hands or smudge as you repeat the mantras that you have decided on. You may be drawn to rattle longer or harder in one area or remain longer over one piece of furniture that another. Go with your intuition. Don't question yourself. Enjoy the process; you are letting go the heaviness from your home and filling it with light.

Step 4. Seal the Space

Having identified and cleared the residual blockages and replaced it with its opposite vibration, it is now time to seal in this new energy. This helps to reconfirm this is what you really want. You are stating that you are ready to live in harmony, abundance, peace, fun, love or whatever your intentions are for your present and future life.

I like to do this using holy water. I bless the corners in each room, starting at the front door and working my way around until I end up back where I started. The mantra I use is *"Bless this space and those who live here, bless this space and all who enter here."* Alternatively, you can picture the house filled with white light. You could ask Archangel Michael to put his cloak of protection down over the property. A friend of mine pictures a ribbon being tied at the front door. Some would invoke the energy of the moon, or the elements. This is going to be your ritual and you will be sealing the space with whatever image is appropriate to your belief system.

Whether you use words, set an intention, use a religious item or a prayer, it is done with complete confidence that your intentions have been heard. The blocked energy has been identified, released and replaced with its opposite. Your home is now like a clean slate ready to start a fresh.

Occasionally we will pick up on more than one type of energy in the same place. Items of furniture may be holding residual energy and at the same time the property can be affected by geopathic energy or there may even be a trapped soul connected to the same property. This has proven to be the case for me on more than one occasion.

Last year I visited friends in Australia. They brought me out to see the Blue Mountain National Park. I had never previously heard of this mountain range. It is a World Heritage site with amazing views. It has the most spectacular scenery and covers a vast area. First, we went to see The Three Sister's rock formations in Katoomba. Having climbed the many steps to the viewing point we then went for a walk in the magnificent forest before heading on to see the mining area.

Some of the old tools used in the mines were on display. For the owners of these tools, these implements would have been precious commodities. As I touched various items, I felt the energy of the original owners, their physical pain, exhaustion, their stooped backs, chest infections, painful knees and shoulders. This was residual energy that I was feeling, memories that had soaked into the metal of the implements as they were held by the same person for long periods of time every day for many months or even years.

While some of the energy I picked up on was residual I was also aware that some of their souls were still earth bound. I asked my friends if they knew why I was seeing the souls of people that looked Asian. They explained that many people had travelled from Asia to Australia to mine that area in the nineteenth century.

This group of ghosts, all male and I struggled to estimate their ages as they were so haggard by years of extreme physical labour. There were some teenage boys among them. I then asked for a passageway to be opened and encouraged these souls to move forward into the light.

One soul approached me and started to speak in his native language. My friend, Mary, tried to do a translation using her phone, as I tried to repeat his words but to no avail. I then asked for this man's higher self to hear me and to communicate through picture and symbols. Through these pictures and my friends' knowledge, we pieced together his story. These men had travelled a seemingly impossible arduous journey, having heard rumours of work in the mines. Some had brought their families with them.

Many of these emigrants had been treated badly. Once they had the hard work done and had found minerals they were sometimes beaten, robbed and even killed. They had paid with their lives for being so successful at their trade. Their dwelling huts were burnt down and their wives and daughters taken to satisfy lust and jealousy. Speaking to his higher self I encouraged him to move forward in the light. I asked his wife and daughter to come forward from the light and accompany him and his son home.

Occasionally I am asked to do a house or land clearance. When I do this work, I aim to identify whether the problem is geopathic, residual or spiritual. Sometimes it is just one of these and sometimes, like my trip to The Blue Mountain National Park, it is a combination.

I am very fortunate to live near The Burren in the West of Ireland. It is a very unique limestone landscape covering approximately 250 square kilometres, often lunar in appearance. The area is famous for its Artic, Alpine and Mediterranean flora, its fauna, its geology and archology. In the mid sixteen-hundreds, while under British rule, an English parliamentarian, Edmund Ludlow, described the area to his colleagues. *"It is a country where there is not enough water to drown a man, wood enough to hang one, nor earth enough to bury him."*

This area was very badly affected by the Great Famine in the 1840's. English rule had seen thousands displaced from their homes on fertile arable land in the East of Ireland and sent to scrape out a living in the poorer lands of the West.

Whenever I do energy work in The Burren, I always assume I will be working on a combination of trapped souls and geopathic stress (as there are so many underground streams and caves in the area). However, this was not the case on one occasion when I was asked to do an energy clearance at a famine village located on a farmer's land. Famine villages are still to be found throughout the West of Ireland, where the entire village was deserted, due to emigration and/or starvation.

The farmer explained that there were two areas in the village that he simply could not go near. The first was by the hedge school (teaching was outlawed under British rule and teachers took to educating the children in areas sheltered by a hedge). The second area he could not enter was the very last house in the village. On approaching either of these sites he would be so overcome with emotion that he had to leave.

His family had lived in the area for many generations and his grandfather had been a child during the famine. Because of this connection, he knew the surnames of the families that had lived in each house. I brought a bag of candles with me. As we entered each ruin, he called the family name and I lit a candle and prayed for the souls of that property. As I started the prayers each family showed me memories from their lifetime. What I hadn't expected was to be shown happy memories. I saw children in their long night shirts getting ready for bed in the open lofts, women sitting by the fire darning socks and men smoking their pipes, often while carving wood. I was shown nothing negative. These souls were all at

156

peace and happy to be remembered, to have their names called and to be prayed for.

We wandered on through the village and came to where the hedge school had been. Immediately I could feel the sadness. I asked my spirit guides to show me where it was coming from. In my mind's eye I could see a young woman. At first, I thought her to be elderly but on looking more intently I could see she was holding her new-born baby. Her clothes were raggedy and her skin tanned from the peat fire, and time spent labouring outside. My guides showed me how she had come to this area every day to cry. She did not want her husband and children to see her distressed and she had put on a brave face while in their company. Every day she would walk down to where the hedge school had previously been held. She would sit and rock her baby and sob her heart out at her inability to feed her family and the decision they faced on emigration. Would her young family survive the voyage, would her husband get work, would they find somewhere to live and what would happen to the relatives she left behind never to see again?

However, her soul was not trapped in this spot, her soul was at peace. The area had held a residual memory of her feelings. The fact that she had come there daily had strengthened the memory. It was as if her tears had soaked into the rock on which she had sat day after day. I asked for white light to surround the area, letting go the sadness and bringing in joy. When I had finished, the farmer walked around the space for the first time in his life without feeling upset.

We balanced precariously on rocks as we crossed over a little stream and continued to the last house in the village. The farmer said he could go no further as he was feeling overwhelmed with emotion, explaining he had on occasion been brought to his knees when he had tried to go into the house. His grandfather had often talked of the elderly couple that lived in the last property in this village. When his grandfather was six years of age, he had discovered their bodies, sitting by the fireplace, holding hands. They had died from starvation. The table was set with plates, cutlery, a jug of water and two mugs. On the plates were pieces of tree bark.

As I connected with the couple, it was the woman's soul who spoke with me. I asked why they had been so badly affected by the famine. She explained their only cow had died, they were too old to emigrate and they did not have children. If they had been blessed with family perhaps their children could have emigrated and sent money home, but this was not to be.

The emotion I felt in that house was complete and absolute love. The pain I felt was her pain for her husband, watching him hungry, searching day after day for something to eat. When he had brought in the pieces of bark, she had set the table the same as every other day, not wanting him to know her distress in case it added to his.

Her pain was mirrored by his, this was the love of his life, his soul mate and he could not provide for her. Each day he watched hopelessly as she got thinner and thinner, weaker and weaker. That night after he had brought in the pieces of bark, she had set the table. Both knew this was their last night and so they sat by the fire, holding hands, looking at the flame until both quietly passed on.

Both souls were completely at peace. They thanked me for my prayers. I asked for light to be put down over their home and replace the pain and hopelessness with new hope and love.

Step 5. Gratitude

This whole process of energy clearing is based on the belief that we are asking an unseen power (though for some of us this may be a seen presence) to:

Hear our request.

Release negativity from our homes

Replace it with whatever energy we now want to live in.

This process is based on a belief that our request will be heard and answered. It is therefore important to acknowledge this assistance and express our gratitude.

"Our contribution to the progress of the world must...

consist of setting our own house in order."

Mahatma Gandhi

SOUL ENERGY

In October 2015 I travelled with two friends to Belgium. My grandfather's cousin, Thomas Sharry, had died near Ypres one hundred years earlier. His family had a farm and a small business in Ireland and his future at home was encouraging. He was an only son. Yet he strongly believed it was the morally correct thing to join the army and help defeat the Germans.

We as a family knew very little about him. I have always had an interest in family history and in my teenage years had done some work on our family tree. Since hearing his name, I had wanted to make the journey to acknowledge him, as no one else from our family had ever gone to visit the memorial site. The only information I had was from the British War Office which stated:

Rank: Rifleman.

Regiment or service: Royal Irish Rifles.

Unit: 1st Battalion.

Date of death: 9 May 1915. Killed in action.

Supplementary information: Born in the Burren, Co. Clare. Enlisted in Liverpool. Son on Michael and C. Sharry, of New Quay, Co Clare, Ireland.

Grave or memorial reference: Panel 9. Memorial: Ploegsteert Memorial in Belgium.

Armed with these few sentences we headed off to find Ploegsteert. It was a beautiful day and even though it was October, the sun was shining in a cloudless sky. On arriving at the monument, I was struck by its vastness. The land was so flat and green. For a man who had never left his home country before, who had lived on a rocky limestone homestead, overlooking the Atlantic Ocean it must have been so strange for him to be here. He had left his native land and became a part of this massive force of soldiers that fought and died in the nearby Ploegsteert Woods. Thousands, including my late cousin, have no grave. Their names are etched in the stone of the monument. This sad fact somehow gave me comfort to know that Thomas who had lived on stone will be permanently remembered on stone.

Having found his name among the thousands of names I was very emotional. Somehow it felt like I was now attending his funeral. I connected with his soul. Thankfully he was at peace in the light. It was very emotional also for Thomas's soul as he connected with me. He was thankful to us for making this journey and that one hundred years after his death he was still remembered by his family.

He then showed me how he died. In my mind's eye I saw a scene unfold. Everywhere was muddy due to the never-ending lines of soldiers and the equipment that they brought by horse and donkey. Walking meant pulling their feet in and out of the sodden earth. Many of the animals lay dead from exhaustion or from gunshot wounds. When the animals died, the soldiers had somehow tried to carry the equipment, while still being shot at. The cannon, which was part of their artillery, was being transported by wooden cart and had become bogged down in the mud. His battalion had taken what little shelter there was in the trees and abandoned the cart in open ground.

Some of the soldiers were assigned to try and free the cannon from the mud. Thomas, who was tall and strong, had been ordered to try to push the cart out of the hole. Walking as far as the cart would have been terrifying as there was no shelter and the condition of the ground made it impossible to make any speedy movement. I saw him pushing the cart, then he was hit by fire from the opposition. I felt a sensation in my legs as I took on a copy of his energy from the event. He must have died instantly. After the initial impact I had no other sensation of pain. I briefly felt intense pain in both legs, then the pain was replaced with a beautiful sense of peace.

Having showed me how he died, Thomas asked me to help two of his comrades who had not crossed over to the light. One name he gave was Rynne and the other was McSweeney. I walked around the monument until I found the Rynne man's name. He also had no grave and the only acknowledgement of his sacrifice was his name etched on stone among the other thousands who died on that hill. I connected with his soul and told him his friend; Thomas Sharry was waiting for him. I said some prayers with him and after a few minutes he moved forward.

I couldn't find the other man's name in the monument. There were plots of graves outside behind the monument and some on the other side of the road. I went to each graveyard and asked to be shown the graves I should stop at. My guides showed me line by line which graves to go to and which souls needed help and were now ready to move forward. I worked my way over and back the lines of graves stopping wherever I was shown a problem. These soldiers had not crossed over for various reasons. Each had their own story. Some had left young wives they had promised to return to and could not accept they would never return and get to keep their promise. Some had been disturbed by the horrors they had seen and participated in; some could not accept any God could exist. Some just couldn't accept this was the end of their life.

I walked across the road and recommenced crossing souls in that graveyard. In the last plot that I entered I asked did anyone need assistance. There was one response. I went over and spoke to the soul and encouraged him to move forward. One of my friends was sitting on the wall patiently waiting for me. He asked what the name was on that grave. I read aloud the name on this headstone. "McSweeney of the Royal Irish Rifles 1st Battalion." This was Thomas's friend whom he had asked me to help. I had become so engrossed in the job at hand going graveyard to graveyard that I had stopped reading the names. As he started to move forward, I could see a woman walk towards him from the light. I presumed she was his wife. Then I saw my cousin Thomas step forward and greet him.

We had travelled all that way for my cousin, and despite his own emotions on the day he had wanted help for his comrades. Even in death he had the same personality and deep belief that we should help those who are in trouble or less fortunate than ourselves. I am very proud to carry his bloodline.

*****

Empaths can pick up on the emotions of others, on geopathic energy and residual energy, now add to this combination the fact that many empaths can also pick up on the presence of Soul Energy.

To understand how this happens we need to come to our own version of the soul's journey and purpose. For me I see the journey as having the following potential steps:

Step 1. Life

Step 2. Trapped Souls/Ghosts

Step 3. The Gate

Step 4. Moving forward in the light

Some of your beliefs may be different to mine, and that is as it should be. We each need to come to our own conclusions on the meaning of life and whether we believe we have a soul and the existence of an afterlife.

Step 1. Life:

I believe we come to this earth to live life to the full and to learn certain lessons. We are born into our family at a specific time and will be impacted by many things including our life experiences, the order we come in the family, family beliefs, our unique DNA, and our personality to be challenged by those lessons.

Step 2. Trapped Souls/Ghosts:

Ghosts have always existed. There are a number of references in the bible. When Jesus walked on water out to the boat where the apostles were, he reassured them that he was not a ghost. Also, after his resurrection he held out his hands for them to touch again telling them he was not a ghost.

These souls have the same personality and the same concerns as they did when they were alive. The difference between them and those that passed on to the light is that these souls are earth-bound. Their movement is slow. Their energy is heavy. They are not meant to be here. It is as if they are fighting gravity, similar to astronauts in outer space.

The vast majority of us on dying pass straight into the light. However, a very small proportion will not take the opportunity to pass on when their time comes. Similar to the infants in the following story. These babies have done no wrong. But some chose for their own personal reasons not to move forward in the light.

THE LITTLE ONES

MARY BURKE

Our visit to two local children's graveyards took place on a cold and wet Sunday morning in December. We had discussed the expedition during group meditation evenings, but I really had no idea what to expect. I knew of one relatively unknown graveyard in a little townland overlooking a wide sweep of bay. From the local maps, I could also see another graveyard listed nearby. This latter site was walled and clearly marked with stones and had a central cross.

Our group consists of seven people who meet weekly, led by Bríd in meditation. We keep in mind various troubled spots locally and historically, and we also pray for healing and wellbeing.

On the Saturday, the day before our visit to the graveyards, I went for a drive in the area and looked at the best access routes to the sites for the group. As I walked towards the first site, I felt nauseas and a heaviness coming over me, despite the beautiful location. I couldn't explain it. However, after leaving the site on that Saturday, I was fine for the rest of the day.

The following morning, we met near the walled graveyard and walked across the fields to the little graveyard. The gate was locked so we remained outside. Bríd lead us in prayers at the wall and around the graveyard, praying for the souls to cross to the light. Bríd had a crystal pendulum which seemed to move on its own energy, spinning at various locations around the site. We prayed for the souls interred at each point. We all sensed different stories of bereaved relatives (usually fathers) bringing their infants to the place of burial. A sense of relief and peace came over me after our prayers.

We drove from there over to the other site. I told Bríd about the heavy sick feeling I experienced on the day before. When we arrived at the little plot we began to pray again in various locations. While we walked around the plot the crystal pendulum which Bríd held started spinning in several places. We prayed for the little souls all around the site, and along the access route, praying for their passing to the light.

We were about finished, and ready to go, in the last round of prayers, when I again had a sense of being drawn to the far side of the site. I could hear inside a little voice saying, "Don't go, don't leave." I told Bríd about this, and we went and prayed on the other side of the site again, and again the crystal (which Bríd held) was whirling around on its own energy. Despite the rain and the cold of the day, we stayed and prayed at the site until peace descended on us. I experienced a real sense of relaxed energy, not the sick sadness that was there before. Everyone had their own story of sensing different traumas at the site.

I must say I had no idea of what we would do on that Sunday, and it was odd to venture out in the rain and wind on a December morning. By the end of our visits to the graveyards, I had a sense of peace and a sense of privilege to have been part of this group, working with Bríd. I am amazed to find that our senses pick up the messages from the spirit world and would never have thought of such strong connection had it not been for my experiences with Bríd. She has an amazing gift, which she shares so readily. I find it comforting to be at ease with the world of the spirit. We fear death, and seldom see it as part of life. I find, through this work with Bríd, that the spirit world provides support and comfort in our daily lives, and we are more connected than we can ever understand. I never cease to be amazed at Bríd's sensitivity to the spirit world and her gift of healing for both the spirit and the physical world.

The children in this story had done no wrong. They were born into a belief system that they could not go to Heaven as they had died before being baptised. They may have sensed their fathers' emotions as they placed their lifeless bodies in little boxes tied to the back of their bikes and cycled with heavy hearts to the site of burial. Not wanting to draw attention to their task, it is unlikely that these men carried a shovel and would have had to dig the grave using a little hand tool or even by hand.

The Catholic Church of the day had forbidden these babies from being buried on holy ground. It was implied that they were not good enough for God to love. Occasionally, even though we don't like to admit it, some of these children had their lives deliberately taken as they were conceived out of wedlock. Various farmers throughout the country had allowed the burials of these babies in designated but unmarked areas on their land. These places were not spoken of aloud, but everyone knew their location. Usually, family members did not return to the burial site because of the stigma attached to the unbaptised infant. However, some of the fathers took a stone from a nearby wall to mark the location where their offspring was now buried. If at a later date, he or the mother of the baby risked returning, they would be able to locate the burial site of their child.

Occasionally, some fathers rebelled against the church rules and under cover of dark buried their little ones in their family plot in their local church grounds. The majority of the children buried at these places had already passed straight to the light at the time of their deaths. Possibly those who had not done so were the very sensitive ones who were more aware of the energy surrounding their deaths. While we worked that morning, I could see couples and family groups of spirits queuing up to bring their children home.

When we pick up on the presence of a trapped soul their energy is generally very cold. The empath with this ability may be able to see the ghost or may see their outline. They may take on the emotional and/or physical pain this soul experienced before their death. For me the easiest way of telling if there is a trapped soul is by paying attention to the temperature in that area. If there is an area in your home that you cannot heat despite adding extra heaters and there is no other obvious explanation, this may be your answer. If, however, you have converted your single block garage into a bedroom it will be colder than the rest of the house. If you have poor insulation or your windows are draughty then that is your answer. The day we went to the graves was wet and cold therefore instead of gauging the temperature I had used a crystal pendulum.

Some empaths feel extreme cold in their hands and feet while the rest of their body is at normal temperature. These sensations may be felt when they are in a certain room or space, or perhaps after visiting somewhere. Others feel a chill across their shoulders. When experiencing this coldness along with emotional or physical pain that is not yours, then the chances are that you are in the presence of a soul that has not passed on.

In the next testimonial, Mary explains how she was picking up on the hunger experienced by a little boy. Once she realised the constant feeling of hunger that she was experiencing was in fact the energy of a soul seeking assistance, she readily agreed to assist me in crossing his soul into the light.

THE FAMINE CHILD

MARY CLARE MCGRATH

Shortly after I arrived in Ireland, I noticed something different about myself. I was constantly eating. Normally, I eat three meals a day, seldom snacking. This went on for several days.

I assigned it to traveling from the USA and having my biological clock off kilter. It didn't rise to the level of talking out loud about it, even to my husband.

I went to see Bríd as I usually do when I am in County Clare. Having said nothing to her about the eating, I lay down on her treatment table. The first question she asked me was, *"Have you been eating a lot since you arrived in Ireland?"* to my astonishment at her question, I replied, *"Yes, I have."*

Bríd went on to tell me, *"There is a soul of an eleven-year-old famine boy outside your house and you are picking up on his hunger."* She describes the pillar in front of my home, which she has never been to, where he was hiding. She said he was afraid to cross over because, during the famine, his parents left their home in search of food, never to return. Before they left, they told him not to leave the house.

Bríd asked me if I would like to help him cross over. I agreed. Bríd led the prayers and the permission for him to cross. I returned to my normal eating patterns, without any urge to eat between meals.

Many times, I have encountered souls from the famine period who had not crossed to the light. Some of these

175

souls were those of children who had not moved forward as they believed they would be disobeying their parents' wishes. Parents and older siblings would have gone out to work on the famine walls and roads while the younger children were left at home and instructed not to leave their house. On dying from starvation while their parents were gone, some of these children did as they were instructed, they did not leave. Others died on the roads; their exhausted ravaged bodies had worked on. Their family's survival depended on them staying alive and working beyond what their failing bodies could endure.

The following story was written by Maureen who is an integral part of our healing meditation circle. If whenever we are working to assist souls to transition there are children involved, they make their way straight for Maureen. She exudes maternal love and they just know they can trust her. This was the case in the following story.

THE FAMINE ROAD

MAUREEN

Bríd has to be one of the most extraordinary women I have ever met. A friend told me about her some four years ago. As soon as I heard about her,

I knew she was one lady I was destined to meet and what a journey it has been. It has taken me ages to write this testimonial, because there has been so much in my amazing journey with this lovely lady, that I could write an entire book about her myself.

There are two particular events on the same theme that I would love to share. I have been very blessed to be part of one of Bríd's weekly meditation groups with six other lovely ladies, all with our own individual gifts and talents with constant encouragement to develop them from Bríd. In these sessions led by Bríd, we direct healing to anyone sick or in need of healing. However, a significant part of our work has been crossing over souls who have not completed their journey to the light for a variety of reasons.

One of the many memorable events was a group walk on Lough Avalla in July 2020. We stopped at the holy well at the start of the walk and prayed for the intentions of the group and those who had requested prayers and healing. Then we continued our walk until we came to the little famine monument halfway up. Bríd suggested we stop and pray for the crossing of any souls who had suffered greatly during this time.

While some in the group would see souls, I would sense them but not always see them. More often than not, those who would come my way for help would be children and animals. When we were standing at the little cairn, Bríd saw a little girl standing beside me tugging on my coat. Her grandmother was with her trying to get her to go but this little sweetheart was looking for her dad as she had died before him. Bríd very successfully connected her with her dad who had been broken-hearted at the loss of his little girl under those circumstances. He had been searching for her too and all three of them went off into the light. The difference in the energy in the place went from heavy to light afterwards and we looked over to see a crew of wild goats standing over by the bushes like they were part of it.

The second event took place on a famine road about two weeks after the Lough Avalla walk. One of the women in our group has serious historical and local knowledge and was very drawn to healing needed in this particular place located at the back of Mulllaghmore. I had never been there before.

The sense of heaviness and sadness as we began to walk along the road was overpowering. Looking on the ground we were walking on, Bríd explained she was shown images of those who worked on the road, men, women and children, having to break the stones with their hands or by using other stones.

We climbed quite a lot of the mountain first and then stopped to have some food. We all connected in and when we were sitting together Bríd brought down Divine white light and proceeded to say the crossing prayers to help the poor souls, many of whom had died during the making of this road. We could see them holding their bleeding hands wrapped in dirty rags, cold, wet and hungry and all for a few shillings to keep their families alive. There were hundreds of souls trying to make their way to the light holding each other, and some barely able to walk.

I had a vision of a well-dressed man on a white horse with a whip trying to block their path. This man was gentry and appeared to be like a landlord. Mary, who was sitting beside me, saw the same man but also a small heavy man slightly bald and sweating, on foot who appeared to be a foreman also trying to stop them. Bríd and the others saw the same vision and it was really clear that these men had been harsh and cruel masters to these poor souls. It began to rain so we made our way back down over some fairly uneven surface but we got there. Ann went over on her ankle and was in quite a lot of pain so we took our time and stopped at the bottom and sat on some large rocks. Bríd again brought down white light, interceded with Archangel Michael to command the two men to step back and allow these souls to pass.

The souls came forward in droves and there were two elderly couples helping each other though barely able to walk. A very thin woman with blonde hair, who looked very unwell came forward and my sense was that she was the wife of the man on the horse. I felt she had been very badly treated by this man during her life. She looked so young but was so happy to go to the light. We continued to send healing until Bríd felt that those who wanted to leave had done so.

We began to walk back towards our cars. I was walking with Mary then, before I knew it, I was flat on my face on top of the jagged stones. It felt like I had been flipped in the air with something holding on to my ankle. The girls were as shocked as I was and I was afraid to move. I got up eventually. One of the girls had seen what looked like a hand coming out of the ground and grab my ankle. It was actually a teenage boy who had been left behind when the other souls had crossed over. He had panicked when we were leaving. Bríd brought down the light again and crossed the lad over with a few more who were stuck. This child had died on the road and was left there and buried under the stones along with many others.

Bríd and the girls channelled healing for myself and Ann (for her ankle) before we left. I actually didn't have any pain whatsoever but I knew I was completely shocked. When I got home, I was distraught that this had happened to this child and was so worried that there were others still there. We did what we could on the day and a return trip may well be needed to complete it.

The moral of this particular story is the need for protection especially for anyone who is an empath, or someone that souls will go to for help. Bríd had explained this so many times before and that it is not alone important to invoke protection before you work with spirit but to disconnect afterwards and return strong in your own energy. I had left my house late that morning and had not invoked any protection whatsoever.

When I got over the shock of the whole thing, I realised that while that boy was reaching out for help in the only way he knew how, he was also teaching me the most important lesson I will ever learn in doing this work. I got a cancellation for my osteopath a few days afterwards as I was convinced that I had injured my neck but thought I was in too much shock to feel the pain. He said that my back was in the best shape he had seen it in for years and that whatever way I fell it looked like I had sorted an underlying back issue – the healing power of the group.

As I said at the start, Bríd is one of the most inspirational women I have ever met. I feel privileged and blessed every day to be part of her crew. I consider the group as my soul buddies whom I will love and cherish. I will be forever grateful to Bríd and to them for the rest of my life for being part of this amazing journey.

Step 3. The Gate:

I picture the soul moving forward from this world to the next and arriving at a gate. With my beliefs this gate is manned by Saint Peter and his staff. Arriving at the gate does not automatically mean we get to pick a cloud and harp to float around on for infinity. This is where we get to assess the life we have lived. It is where we look at our actions, inactions and interactions during our lifetime. From my experiences with departing souls, I have always seen loved ones come forward from the light and make their presence known to the person who is dying. Sometimes the dying person is aware of the presence of their loved ones for a number of days before it is their time to join them. The same is true for souls that have been earth-bound and are finally ready to move forward; they also will be accompanied by loved ones.

On rare occasions the departing soul will not have loved ones already in light. Perhaps they have been disconnected from family. If a young person is about to depart, they may not know anyone who has died as their parents and grandparents are still alive. In these instances, I have seen angels coming forward and in one case I have seen Mother Mary coming to bring a little girl home to the light. The little girl did not know anyone who had died but she was familiar with seeing statues and pictures of Mother Mary and was happy to go with her.

Step 4. Moving forward in the light

Once we have transitioned to the light, with the help of our loved ones, our guides and angels we start to review the life that we have lived. Here we look at how we treated others. We look back at the lessons we were meant to learn and see what progress we made. This is done in a loving and encouraging way. For me, this part of the process is like finishing secondary school or college. We will have received grades in various subjects reflecting how much effort we put in. Some subjects will have been easier than others and some harder.

If we were born into an affluent family, giving to charity may have been easier for us than for those who were marginalised by society or lived lives of poverty. Yet someone may have made wealth their focus in life and believed their status made them more important. Someone living a life of poverty may have stolen food to survive or in order to keep their family alive. Yet this person may have been more generous with what little they had and also more generous with their time and words of encouragement.

As we analyse the life we lived, we begin to accept our shortcomings. We start to forgive those we believe

184

did us wrong and we see the bigger picture. We come to a point where we can forgive ourselves for the wrongs that we have done others. We reach an understanding of our experiences and what had led us to doing those wrongs.

Often souls that are moving forward in the light will visit their loved ones who are still alive. This is very different to those souls who are earth-bound. These souls are in the light. Their energy is lighter, they are not fighting gravity and there is no change in temperature.

One client has frequently seen orbs of light on her baby monitor. When I asked her guides to explain who was visiting the house, they described various relatives who have died, giving their names and some unique information. These souls are at peace, yet even though they have never known their grandchild or grandniece in this life they still love her and want to check in on her and offer love and support. Also, young children often have the ability to see spirits and angels. Most of us will have seen babies and young children staring at 'nothing' and smiling.

During many of my client sessions, souls from the light have come forward to let the client know they are okay and that they have made it home. They still love and support their family here on Earth. Sometimes they will have specific things to say that will bring closure and help their family members move forward. While other times the evidence that their souls continue on and the knowledge that the bonds of love remain unaltered, is healing in itself.

BIG LOVE, BIG LOSS
ANONYMOUS

I had read Bríd's book, *Memories And Missions*, and I enjoyed it immensely. My friend suggested we make an appointment to visit Bríd. I was looking forward to meeting her in person. But on the morning that we were scheduled to visit, I awoke with a very sore ankle. It was hard to walk on it that day. I had previously fractured it. When we arrived at Bríd's house, she greeted us warmly and she immediately felt the pain I had in my foot.

When I entered the healing room, Bríd told me that I came with my dad's spirit. It was just approaching my dad's second anniversary and I had found it a very difficult time. I had been grieving silently since my dad's passing that I didn't really speak about it to anyone. Bríd picked up on this. She described my dad as only I would have known. She acknowledged the strong bond, love and friendship we had. Bríd lit a candle and prayed for healing. I felt a deep inner peace come over me as she prayed. It was as if time and the world stood still in that room. On leaving, Bríd left me with this special message:*"Big love, Big loss."* Meeting Bríd that day was a huge turning point for me in healing from the heartache of my dad's passing to the spirit world. I'm grateful to her, as that peace has stayed with me ever since that visit.

I walked out of her house also pain-free in my ankle too. I really believe my ankle acted up that morning to give me a physical sign of Bríd working as a truly gifted healer.

FOLLOW THE LEADER

As children we played a game called Follow the Leader. One child would be chosen as the leader and the other children had to follow their instructions. "Hop on one leg – stop." As the instruction to stop was issued we would stand as still as statues in whatever position we were in at the time. *"Pretend you are a train – stop, spin in a circle – stop, run as fast as you can – stop, march like a soldier – stop."* During the game the only person allowed speak was the leader.

As adults we can find ourselves in similar circumstances, with the appointed leader issuing instructions. No one else is allowed to speak or offer their opinion. We follow on like sheep. Sometimes the rules don't sit well with us, but we still follow along. Similarly, when we join a work force our new manager/supervisor explains our duties and terms of employment. We are informed of the company's policies: environmental, confidentiality, equal opportunities and health and safety etc. The Revenue Commissioners sets the rules on the financial contributions we must pay in taxes. The Department of Enterprise, Trade and Employment sets out our legal entitlements. One would think that armed with all these policies we would all find ourselves in a safe and pleasant environment. Unfortunately, this is not always the case. The work environment is impacted by the personalities of those who work there.

If those in leadership roles are hardworking, caring and respectful of their staff, this will ripple down positively through the company. Individuals who feel appreciated and valued will be happy to work hard and give back this respect to their managers. However, if those in management/supervisory positions are driven by ego, the knock-on effect on staff will be fear, resentment and frustration.

It can be very difficult to take a stand against what we believe to be unjust, especially if everyone else is prepared to follow the leader. We look back on events in World War I and II and wonder how did it happen? How did so many follow orders and commit atrocities? However, we also hear many heroic stories of those who did not follow blindly along, of those who did what they could to save as many as possible. Yet now in our advanced twentieth century as we watch our TV's we are made aware that genocide and other outrages continues to occur in many parts of our world. Atrocities have happened in every country. Somehow these atrocities are harder to accept when occasionally world leaders, through their ego, are partly responsible for the outcome.

The personal characteristic whereby some are drawn to be leaders out of ego instead of working for the greater good has existed since time began. Often, we see people in the top roles in all walks of life, who are led by ego. They believe their actions are unquestionable and that they are automatically deserving of respect.

In the New Testament – Luke 20:46 (Living Bible Edition) – Jesus discusses this very topic.

"Beware of these experts in religion, for they love to parade in dignified robes and to be bowed to by the people as they walk along the street.

And how they love the seats of honour in the synagogues and at religious festivals!

But even while they are praying long prayers with great outward piety, they are planning to cheat widows out of their property.

Therefore, God's heaviest sentence awaits these men."

The consequences of our action or inaction weigh differently on each of us depending on our individual life story. I have been privileged to visit some of the war fields of World War I and II. Like many empaths I have the ability to feel the emotional and physical pain of souls who have not crossed on to the light. When doing this type of work, I ask my guides to only allow those souls who are ready to transition to come forward for assistance. As I travelled through war fields, each soul I encountered had a unique story which was stopping their progression.

Some had promised loved ones they would return home. As I stood by the grave of one of these soldiers, I couldn't feel any physical pain, I realised he had died instantly from his injury. But I did feel his heartache, I encouraged him to move forward and invited his loved ones in spirit to come forward and bring him home. His wife stepped forward; she placed his baby in his arms. His son who he had never met, had not been born when his father went to war. I watched as this baby grew to a young boy, then continued to change and grow until he became an elderly man, now also deceased. The young soldier took the hand of his wife and son and walked forward into a magnificent light.

Other souls I met had regretted killing, even though they had been conscripted. Prior to the war many had been farmers, labours or factory workers who loved all life. Their choice on the battel field was to kill or be killed. Some had committed atrocities. One young German soul showed me some of the inhumane actions he had carried out. He had joined Hitler's Youths at seven and been completely brainwashed.

All these souls were young men when they died. I felt their physical injuries, their mental and emotional turmoil. I spoke with each soul I encountered; some needed to tell their story. I prayed with and for each of them, while asking for a passageway to open and bring them home. I then asked to be disconnected from their energy as I handed their soul's progression over to a higher power.

In May 2012 I travelled with a tour group to Gallipoli, Turkey. One of the places on our itinerary was Suvla Bay and the graveyards in the surrounding area. In August 1915 thousands of troops under British command landed here. This landing was part of the offensive to finally break the deadlock of the Battle of Gallipoli. It resulted in casualties from both sides totalling in excess of forty thousand young men.

We went to Suvla Bay first, before going on to visit some of the nearby graveyards. I had started to mentally prepare myself before reaching the bay for the bombardment of emotions I expected to feel on getting there. Thankfully, this was not the case. The bay felt peaceful and still. I realised that numerous religious services have been held here since the war bringing healing to the area and assisting the souls to traverse. I had a completely different experience here to what I had expected. I was able to stand on the shoreline and rejuvenate my energy and settle my thoughts before proceeding to the graveyards.

We got back on the bus and travelled on to the graveyards. Our journey up the mountain pass was like no other I had experienced. On every side of us there were graveyards. It is believed that approximately one hundred and forty-seven thousand young soldiers lost their lives in this mountainous area. I prayed as we drove past them for light to be put down over the mountain and for passageways to be opened for any souls ready to travel on to the light. I asked my angels that I would be directed to the graves of the souls who were most in need of my assistance. As I walked among the graves, I saw the souls of many young men who were ready to move forward in the light. Some moved on as soon as a passageway was opened. Others needed to tell their story or give their reason for not transitioning.

I was particularly touched by the actions of the soul of a British officer, who even in death still cared for his men. He directed the souls of his soldiers who were now ready to transition to present themselves to me in an orderly queue. He placed two young medics at the front of the queue. They looked so young I presumed they had lied about their age when enrolling. These teenage boys had died terrified and in shock at the horrors they had encountered and the impossible weight of responsibility placed on their young shoulders.

Being so young and with no experience using a rifle, their Officer was concerned that they would not be able to participate in the line of fire. Instead, he appointed them as medics. Without any formal training, they were supposed to care for the injured and carry the never-ending number of maimed bodies off the battlefield. Despite their young years they had both given their all in their attempts to care for the wounded. This same Officer who had tried to keep them from the line of fire now wanted them to be attended to first. Even in death this Officer felt the responsibility of caring for his men and to do his best by each of them.

*****

When I encounter souls, they always come with their own unique individual personality that they had in life. They have the same sense of humour, (or not) and still feel the same care for their loved ones. Walking through the rows of graves I empathically felt the physical pain experienced by the soldiers as they died. I also empathically felt their emotions: anger, fear, loss and confusion. These feelings helped me understand why some had not crossed on. I was able to use this information as I communicated with them, saying sentences relevant to each soldier: *"Let go your fear, the war is now over" "The war is over, go to the light" "Let go your grief, your loved ones await you in the light."*

SEVEN STEPS

I have developed a simple, yet very effective way of disconnecting from the energy of others, while using my empathic ability for the greater good.

At first, I really had to work on this and continuously remind myself to check in. Thankfully, I have very good friends who now also have a much better understanding of me and my frequent journeys into the emotions of others. These close friends are now able to let me know if they think I am acting out of character when they believe I am not myself!

These are the steps that have empowered me. By using these I get to be the person I was always meant to be while still helping others.

1. **Tune in.**
2. **Check in.**
3. **Identify.**
4. **Get help.**
5. **Disconnect.**
6. **Return to own energy.**
7. **Gratitude.**

Step 1. Tune in.

As I wake each morning, I tune into myself and see how I am feeling. Perhaps my answer is that I slept well, feel rested and ready for the day. Or maybe I slept badly and am really anxious about something I have to do today. Perhaps I am concerned for a loved one. This is me; these are my feelings. This is now my base line for the day.

This might sound unnecessary or even ridiculous, but for most empaths this is possibly the single most important action. Many of us will have spent huge parts of our lives *not feeling ourselves* or not knowing our own feelings. We need to take it back to basics. **How do I feel?**

Step 2. Check in.

Throughout the day I regularly check in with myself and see how I am feeling. It has been a new experience for me to name emotions, but it really helps me identify what's going on. I name how I am feeling; anxious, sad, tired, etc., I then ask myself if this emotion is in proportion to my day. Has something happened to me since I got out of bed to explain why I feel like this? When the answer is *yes*, then this is mine and I can deal with it appropriately (or not!). If, however, it is not in proportion to my day, then I know that I have stepped into a copy of someone else's emotions.

This is what I explained to Colette, a lady who came to see me recently. I told her that she is an empath and explained how this can affects her daily life. As she started to comprehend this information, she had some moments of realisation. Colette recalled being out shopping in town on a busy afternoon. While in the department store, she saw a neighbour shopping with her young daughter. Colette stopped to say a polite hello. She didn't know them very well, just in a friendly neighbourly way. As Colette started speaking to her neighbour, she found herself overwhelmed with feelings of guilt, anxiety and sadness. She was struggling not to cry.

After some general conversation the young mum explained to Colette that she was on her way home from a hospital appointment where her little girl had been diagnosed as being on the autistic spectrum. Colette started crying. The mum and child quickly said their goodbyes and moved on.

While Colette was reflecting on the day, she now understood her reactions. The guilt, anxiety and sadness were all copies of the young mum's feelings. They were not Colette's emotions. In that moment she was experiencing her neighbour's guilt for how she had reprimanded the child, not understanding the little girl's difficulties, her anxiety about how she would cope and her sadness for the limitations this could put on her daughter's opportunities in life.

By going into the copy of her neighbour's energy, Colette was absolutely of no assistance. If she understood her empathic abilities and had some knowledge on how to disconnect, the outcome could have been very different. She could have offered to go for a cup of tea and provided a compassionate ear to listen to the woman's story. Or perhaps she could have helped to look up information on the internet, or maybe volunteered her services as an occasional child-minder. Instead, now any time the mother sees Colette she quickly moves on and tries to avoid making eye contact with her.

Step 3. Identify

Having identified the emotions that are not mine I try to work out if I know who they belong to. When I ask this question, I usually have a picture flash in front of me of the person in emotional turmoil. Sometimes it's really obvious. We might observe how our behaviour changes when in the company of certain work colleagues, or when we visit a certain relative.

Sometimes it can belong to someone that we have not yet met but will soon be in their company. This is what happened in my encounter with the manager who was flustered and was dropping things. This was also apparent in the story of the angry man, whose energy had consumed me to the point of considering throwing the car navigation system through the windscreen. I had yet to physically meet these people but I was already aware of them energetically. Even from a distance I had been affected by their emotional distress and I had unknowingly taken on a copy of their emotions.

Occasionally it can be someone who we will not physically come into contact with, but we are very connected to emotionally. If there is someone with whom we have a strong bond, even if they are in a different part of the country or even in a different country, we have the ability to feel their feelings. This is what happened to me with my youngest sister, who lives in Australia. On both occasions when she was in labour,

I felt contraction pain even though she had not phoned me to say her babies were on their way.

Many of us will feel intuitively that we need to phone a loved one and on doing so we find they are experiencing some difficulty. Or if a family member is ill in hospital, we can exhibit some of their symptoms. We can perhaps feel some of their physical pains or their exhaustion and anxiety. The sooner we can identify that these feelings are not ours the better for everyone.

There have been occasions when I have not been able to identify who owns the symptoms. This is particularly the case when the emotions belong to someone I have not yet met. Sometimes we have to think outside the normal answers to include all those we have a strong bond with.

BISCUIT

MARIA

Trying to cut the lawn turned out to be a huge challenging task for me the other day. Thankfully, I wasn't in a rush due to the lock down of Covid19 and I had all the time in the world. We live on a half-acre site and normally one of the kids would do the mowing, but something was telling me to do it this time. So off I went with the lawn mower and started to potter away, on this beautiful sunny day.

Now looking back, of course I was being told by the Divine to do it as yet another learning opportunity for me, but more about that in a minute. You see I've been going to Bríd for many years now and she's told me I'm an Empath, which I completely believe. However, there is a tiny voice inside of me at times that goes *"Really?? Really can that be. Is it all nuts?"* Well, when I tell you what happened when I was mowing the lawn *'really'* happened to me, you will understand why I am smiling since.

There I am in the garden bombing around happy out. All is great in my world until the container for the grass needed emptying. I bent down and I got the most immense pain in my abdomen, out of nowhere, weird, as I was feeling fine and when I stood up straight it went. Everything was fine again until the next time I went to empty the lawn mower and there it was again, severe pain. Weird, eh?

Well, I thought I was going nuts as the pain was strange to say the least. This went on for about three hours. As I said, I was in no rush.

I finished up and started tidying everything away. I had gone into the garage and one of Bríd's questions popped into my head. *"Was this my pain?"* Literally as the words came in it was followed by *"No."* Wow I thought that was strong and before I asked the next question I was smiling as I felt I already knew the answer. So, I asked, *"Whose pain is this?"* and then Biscuit came into my head. Biscuit is my dog of nearly nine years and we had only found out two weeks previous that she was pregnant. *"NO"* I thought *"Could it be? Could I be picking up on her contractions"?* Now I was bent over with laughter. I thought I was nuts.

Later that evening Bríd happened to phone me. Divine timing as always. I asked her the question, could I have been picking up on Biscuits stuff to which she replied *"Yes."* I work as a therapist and had treated Biscuit a few times that week. Bríd explained that I hadn't disconnected from Biscuit's energy and therefore was still attached and feeling her pains. I was blown away by this, it was so strong and powerful it was unreal. Another fantastic lesson learnt.

Biscuit went on to have eight beautiful healthy puppies that night. Thank God I disconnected when I did is all I say and thank God Bríd rang.

Step 4. Get help:

On working out that someone is in emotional turmoil I silently ask for Divine and angelic assistance for that person. If I know who is in trouble, I will say something like *"Please help Sally in her grief" "Surround Tony in healing light"* or otherwise something like *"Please help whoever owns this anger"* or *"Please help whoever is connecting with me at this time."* Over the years I have learnt that God knows more than I do! Originally, when calling in light I used to be very specific and tell God exactly what needed to be done. I now know that once the basic request is put in, it is between God and the person in trouble to work through the situation. I request that the outcome be for the greater good. We may not like the outcome or understand it, but likewise we do not know the bigger picture. Once we have called for help, we have to hand it over.

I think of it as being similar to seeing a building on fire and calling the fire brigade. When the fire brigade turns up, we don't tell them how to do their job, or which end of the building to start working in. Nor do we follow them around the burning building to check up on them and make sure that they are doing it correctly. They are trained, this is their responsibility and we need to let them get on with it.

The person we are requesting assistance for, has the right to decide if they want things to change. When I started out working as a healer I was asked to call to the home of an elderly woman in my neighbourhood. The first time I called I identified her arthritic pains in her joints and her lack of energy. I asked for healing for these areas. She was delighted with my visit and I agreed to check in on her the following week.

Returning a week later, I noticed a considerable level of healing had been received by her body and I happily told her how much more flexible her joints seemed. The old woman's body stiffened. This was news she was not happy to hear and definitely not happy to hear while her daughter-in-law was present. I was confused but said nothing further about it and made polite conversation about the weather.

On visiting her on a third occasion I noticed no further improvements. If anything, the severity of her symptoms had returned almost to the level they were at during my first visit. I sympathised with her and her levels of pain. Her face lit up and she seemed to be genuinely delighted with the outcome.

Back at my own house later that evening I tried to make sense of what was happening. This elderly woman lived alone. When she was ill or in pain her family members called to visit more frequently. Neighbours helped with chores. Her niece slept over more often. She received daily phone calls from her sister. All were concerned for her wellbeing. When she was more capable this assistance was less available. The woman was afraid to heal. She didn't like being on her own. I learnt so much from her. Up to this point, I had thought everyone wanted to be well and be able to live their life to the full. I had never considered that people were afraid to get well.

This experience helped me understand what was going on with a young man in his mid-twenties who I met some years later. He was suffering from depression and was occasionally self-harming. He had lived on his own briefly but had, at the suggestion of his parents, moved back home. He had never been able to hold down employment for any significant period of time.

As I worked with this man, I was able to understand his anxiety around getting well. He was afraid that he would have to move out and live on his own. Afraid of having to find work and provide for himself. He had come to a place of safety, being cared for and provided for by others and did not trust his ability to live independently. He was afraid of being well. I discussed these fears with him. Just by naming this belief allowed him to bring his awareness to it and to look at his situation differently.

We discussed some of the many things he could do and participate in if his health improved. We looked at ways that he could start to incorporate some of these into his current life in an easy way. Perhaps he could do an on-line course instead of having to face the pressure involved in returning to education in a formal classroom setting. I suggested he take on some more household tasks, that he could prepare lunch for himself and his parents. If he started with these small steps the bigger steps may seem less challenging. Yet ultimately, all these decisions were his to make. When calling in assistance for this young man, my request was for whatever help was for his highest good and for whatever assistance he felt safe accepting.

Step 5. Disconnect

Having called in assistance for the person in emotional or physical pain there is nothing to be gained by remaining in a copy of their energy for a moment longer. We have felt their pain, we have called for help and now it is in everyone's best interest that we remove the copy of their energy. It is now time to take off their *borrowed sweater*. There are lots of different ways of doing this. The simpler the technique you choose the better. It is the intention that will make the difference.

I encourage clients to come to simple and discrete techniques for disconnecting from the energy of others. This can be wiping our hands on our jeans or sweater as if we are dusting something off or rubbing our hands together. It can be through visualisation, perhaps picturing a bubble around yourself or a cape being zipped up around you. If you are someone who has a relationship with Archangel Michael, perhaps you could visualise him using his sword to separate your energy from the other person or situation.

Whatever method we choose we are setting a belief in our mind that when we do this it switches off our connection, similar to turning on and off the light switch in our kitchen. I would suggest you put some thought into this before adopting it. Make sure it's easy, quick, and available. I used to think that I had to wash my hands in order to disconnect. If we make the process into a big production of hopping backwards on one foot while chanting, it could cause lots of embarrassing moments. If we are picking up on any external energy while going about our daily lives, like while shopping, the quicker and more discrete the method that we have chosen for disconnecting the better.

A man who attended one of my workshops had developed a system whereby whenever he realised that he was picking up on emotional pain of another, he would get a mass said for that person's intentions. I explained to him that until such time as he got this organised, he was still in a copy of the other persons emotions. This meant that he could often spend days or even weeks feeling the pain and distress of another. If he still felt the need to get a mass said then yes of course he should do so. However, he should disconnect from their energy as soon as he realised that he was in a photocopy of emotions that were not his. I reminded him that the longer he took to disconnect, the more all those who came into contact with him, including his family, would be impacted by his *new behaviour*. The faster we can identify and disconnect the better for everyone.

Step 6. Return to own energy.

Having disconnected we now need to come back solidly into our own energy. Otherwise, we can be left in 'no man's land'. I think of this phase as similar to sheets blowing on a clothesline on a windy day. We are still not at our best, not grounded, not focused on our own day, our own tasks and challenges. Again, whatever system we adopt doesn't matter, it's the intention that will make the difference.

Personally, I take two deep breaths. As I take the first breath, I really bring my attention to the breath and observe it as it comes all the way into my lungs. With the second breath I imagine it coming all the way down through my body to my feet. I feel my feet making contact with the earth. While taking the first breath I am silently state *"I return to my own energy"* and with the second breath *"I return solid in my own body."*

Having something to eat or drink can also help us feel grounded. I went through a phase of having something to eat after every client I worked with. Yes, I certainly felt grounded but I also put on weight. Whatever system you put in place can be amended or changed until you find a way that works for you. This will enable you to really feel like yourself, so that you are solid, present and able to participate fully in your own life.

Step 7. Express gratitude

For me, expressing gratitude to whatever higher power we have called on for assistance is equally important as the previous six steps. Having gone through the steps in the process I always say *"Thank you"* to the Divine and all others from the angelic and spiritual realms that have answered my requests.

As children we are thought that when someone helps us, we should always say *"Thank you."* If we are ungrateful or selfish, expecting that it is our right to be always taken care of and always having our needs met without appreciation, we may find help is slower to come, and that people are not as friendly towards us. The same applies to prayer. If we just ask repeatedly, " *I want, I need, get me, teach me, guide me, help me, help them, disconnect me, keep me safe"* with no appreciation, then things may not always flow as smoothly as we would like.

Recently a cousin shared a story with me that he had been told about Heaven. The storyteller had a dream that an angel was showing them around Heaven. First, they went into a very busy workroom filled with angels. The angel explains *"This is the Receiving Section. Here, all petitions to God are received and sorted."* This room had lots of activity, sorting petitions from people all over the world.

Then they moved down a long passageway to a second room. On the entrance it had a sign with the words *Packaging and Delivery Section*. This is where the blessings and intersessions the people asked for are processed and delivered. This was again an extremely busy workstation. So many blessings had been granted and were now being packaged and delivered.

Finally, at the farthest end of the passageway was a very small room. Inside there was only one angel siting silently. On the door the sign read *Acknowledgment Section*. The single member of staff explained that after people receive the blessings they requested, very few send back acknowledgements. The storyteller asked their angel *"How does one acknowledge God's blessings and assistance?"* *"Simple"* The angel answered, *"Just say, Thank You."*

If we follow these steps, we can let go our fears of meeting a negative person, or that something bad will happen if we have run out of sage!

1. **Tune in** – *"How do I feel today?"*

2. **Check in** – **During the day repeat the question** *"How do I feel now, are my feelings in proportion to the events of my day?"*

3. **Identify** – *"If these feelings are not mine, do I know to who they belong to?"*

4. **Get help** – **Ask for Divine/angelic/universal or spiritual assistance for whoever owns the emotion you are picking up on.**

5. **Disconnect** – **Perform your chosen symbol e.g., rubbing hands together,** *"I ask to be disconnected."*

6. **Return to own energy** – **Take two breaths,** *"I return to my own energy"* **and with the second breath** *"I return solid in my own body."*

7. **Gratitude** – *"Thank You."*

We can also introduce random rituals into our life. I incorporate rituals into my weekly routine. I think of this as spring cleaning my energy field. Pick something you like to do:

Have an extra-long soak in the tub or extra time in the shower. I set the intention that *I am letting go all energy other than my own* and imagine it being washed away.

Maybe you like to get fresh air; as you step into the garden or balcony, or as part of your walk or cycle, you could set your intention that *the wind blows away all negativity*.

If you are fortunate to live somewhere warm, then you could set the intention that *the sun melts away all energy other than yours*, leaving you refreshed and reenergised.

Some people frequently cleanse their energy by using sage or incense or with sound. All methods are perfect as long as you are stating your intention for this cleansing process. Ask to *be released from all energy other than your own* while taking your bath or shower, or during out-door activities, using sage or whatever feels right to you. I have been asked by clients *"I take showers all the time. Why am I still in the energy of others?"* or *"I frequently sage my home. Why isn't the heaviness lifting?"* We need to set our intention.

If you were to go into a grocery store and give the owner twenty euro, the store owner will have no idea what you want. Yes, they will guess you want something they sell in their store but without a clear request or shopping list they will not know what to give you in exchange for the money. Similarly, when using sage to clear your home, if all you are doing is smudging it in every room and every corner without clearly working out your intention of what energy you want released and what type of energy you want to replace it with, nothing will change. The only difference is that now your home smells of sage!

By knowing that we have the psychic codes within ourselves to deal with whatever we pick up on we can let go our fears. We have the ability to disconnect and return strong in our own energy, while calling in light for a struggling person or situation. We can wear our labels with pride. The majority of our time can now be spent solely being ourselves. When we embrace our ability and incorporate our new codes, the transformation in our life is a joy for all who know us. That said, it takes work and persistence. This is exactly what Rowyn did as she took back her power. She has gone on to live a happier and

215

healthier life. I am very proud of this teenage empath and the transition she has made.

THE YOUNG EMPATH

ROWYN

I had to learn from an early age that being an empath could have many effects on me. By attending Bríd's classes and having treatments, I was able to figure out what emotions were mine and what I was picking up from people in my company, especially my friends. Picking up on the emotions of others made me feel unwell and down. But learning techniques and tools to understand and separate things has helped me to live a healthier lifestyle.

Things still affect me from time to time but I no longer feel as overwhelmed by them. It is important to understand that life is challenging but there are ways to make things easier for myself.

It can be hard to make friends and keep them when you are sensitive to people's energies. I feel many people my age just do not understand the impact it has on me. I can feel quite drained at times, but this is when I turn to others who understand for help.

I am grateful for the support I have and I know that this is teaching me to help people like me when I'm a little older. I am excited for that.

Thank you Bríd x

Using my steps, I am no longer in fear of picking up on the emotions of others. I know that when I do, I can disconnect, and also do some good. However, there are occasions when we are completely overwhelmed with emotion to the point where we can hardly function. In this space it will be very difficult, if not impossible, to remind ourselves of all seven steps. The most important thing to remember is to ask to *be disconnected from the energy of all others and to return/remain solid in our own energy*. There may be times when all we can manage is self-preservation, then that is what is important. In these circumstances if we can remember to take our two breaths, we will be stronger in ourselves. We are of no use to anyone if we break.

PROTECTION

Those who are sensitive tend to be the big-hearted people, who will do whatever they possibly can for others. If it was within our human capacity to head off with a wheelbarrow and actually collect the emotional and/or physical pain of others, to put their pain in our wheelbarrow, we would happily push it up the hill for them. But that is not what we are being asked to do. It is their pain, their personal cross and their life lessons to carry. Yes, we can call in help for them. We can walk up the hill beside them and cheer them on. We can be their friend. But we must allow everyone to be responsible for what is in their own wheelbarrow.

We have to learn that we are worth minding, that our needs are important and that we are personally responsible for our physical and mental health. When we are weighed down by the concerns of others we are not participating fully in our own lives. We are not on top of our game. If we compare ourselves to members of a top rugby team, within that team there are loose-head and tight-head props, hookers, flankers, wing forwards, fly half and various other roles, including coaches, managers, all the way to the person who washes the kit.

Each team member is working to the best of their ability, each with a different role and a different job.

When a player is not at the top of their game they will be taken off, put on the bench and substituted. Their replacement, though playing in the exact same position, will play their game differently, yet to the best of their unique ability. If we are the fly half and worried so much about the loose-head prop that we are not doing our job and possibly hindering them from doing theirs, it's just not going to work. We have to play our own position.

If a company has an amazing staff member who is exceptional at their job, they will really want to keep, train and encourage this person. However, if the employee is not taking care of themselves - not switching off, not taking breaks, getting over involved in the workload of others, unable to concentrate, tired, possibly slipping in and out of emotional states - the company will have to look to recruit someone else. It is the same with us. I think of empaths as staff members of a higher power with a capacity to do endless good. If we are not practicing self-care and following our steps, we will end up on the bench. We will not be capable of achieving our full potential.

It can be challenging for some to think of *I* rather than *We*. For much of the time we are slipping in and out of other people's energy and especially the energy of our loved ones. We have become conditioned to making our choices based on *We* rather than *I*. Many of us have yet to learn who *I* really am. What do *I* love doing? What is *my* favourite place to visit? What is *my* opinion? We have spent so many years answering in the plural that it is almost frightening to answer just for ourselves and in line with our own true feelings.

I'm not suggesting that we all turn into high maintenance divas. That's very different from truly embracing the belief that our opinion matters. Many of us will have to take this gradually as we learn who we really are and learn to tune into our gut and be guided by it. As we learn to self-care and speak on our own behalf, we become much more our own person.

It is important that we take care of our physical and mental health. Our wellbeing in turn impacts on our spiritual connection. When we are mentally and physically well, we perform at the top of our game. When we pick up on energy outside of ourselves it will be more obvious if we are strong in ourselves. By following our steps, we will do our job as empaths and then return to our own energy without collateral damage.

This is definitely preferable to being unpredictable and behaving like someone with multiple personalities. By practicing healthy boundaries and being true to ourselves we will be much more likely to live our lives to the full. *When* we are practicing selfcare and accept our ability, we can start to see the magic that is occurring all around us.

MAGIC

RUTH HOLLINGSWORTH

I don't remember when I first realised that I was sensitive to energies. In my teens, I knew I could use my hands to alleviate headaches from friends, especially my best friend. I would call her if I had a headache (which I don't often suffer from), only to find out she had a headache, or a stomach-ache which I didn't think was to do with me; she would have a stomach-ache and I could hold my hands over the area and the pain would go away. The energy is not from me but channelled through me somehow.

In more recent years, I had morning sickness for two weeks, before the same friend told me she was pregnant and had been suffering terribly with morning sickness. I explained my 'symptoms', it was exactly what her body was going through.

I've also experienced holding someone's jewellery and being able to hone into what the item meant to the person and when she wore it. Having said that, I described what I felt and she then explained what that meant to her and how accurate my feelings were. I wouldn't have been able to interpret what the item meant to her; I could only describe what I felt when I held it.

Before I moved to Ireland from the UK some ten years ago, I used to hear mumbling voices in the background. I can only describe as being on a different energy plane because they weren't out loud and I wouldn't describe it as in my head. I would know the dynamics of the voices i.e., if it was a father and a son or a gaggle of women. They were never aware of my presence; I could never hear the particulars of what was being said but I was never bothered by it. On the odd occasion, I will hear a voice loudly shout something in the physical plane, just one word and always when I am on my own with no-one else around. That always startles me. When I moved to Ireland, I could still feel energy very strongly surrounding others and often through my hands but I stopped 'hearing' things.

Last year Bríd invited me into a meditation circle, which has since opened old and new doors for me. Being in a space with like-minded people has restored my sensitivities and made me feel fully myself again. During one of our guided meditations, Bríd took us to our safe space and invited us to open the doors for anyone in our lives who needed healing to come in. Naturally I asked my Mum in. She had just had a serious bout of flu followed by pneumonia. Funny thing was, before I could even envisage my Mum, this old man turned up, stood there in his farming clothes - old 'suit' trousers for want of a better description, a matching jacket, white shirt and cap. This gentleman was grinning at me and I knew instantly that it was my friend's Uncle Willy, whom I don't know and have never met. My friend has talked about Uncle Willy many times so I was aware of his trips in and out of respite due to his health and age.

The following day, I spoke to my friend and told her about my experience. I told her I thought perhaps she should call him, to check he was okay and asked her if I could see a picture of him. On seeing a picture of this man, I have no doubt it was him. My friend called in on him the following morning to see how he was doing in respite. She reported that he was in 'flying form', a good visit by all accounts.

That same night, he passed away peacefully in his sleep. It wasn't until my friend pointed out to me the significance of my experience and her seeing her uncle on the day of his passing that I realised his visitation was to prompt her, to say her farewells. Unbeknownst to me, my friend had herself wondered if she was holding her Uncle back energetically (this was after my talking to her). She went on to visually cutting the energetic cords between herself and her uncle.

Magic... Thank you, Bríd for helping me to open up again and feel what is going on around me in a more fulfilling way.

Tip for redirecting energy

This is an additional technique that I have developed over the years. There are some people in life who seem to permanently be in *poor me* mode. I don't mean those who genuinely have experienced grief or are ill or in pain. I mean those who will tell us repeatedly the wrongs their neighbour or ex-boyfriend did to them ten years previously. When we are in their company for any length of time, we can literally feel like they have drained the life out of us. On leaving their company we want to crawl home and nap. Meanwhile they feel reenergised after the conversation and our sympathetic ear. We are literally allowing them to recharge using our battery, but this leaves our battery flat.

This does neither person any good. The *poor me* individual learns to feel good when they are rehashing the injustices of life, while we are good for nothing after allowing this to happen. When in their company, if I feel my energy being drained, I turn my foot towards the door with the intention that their energy will bounce off my energy field and be directed outside. I then ask silently for light to surround this individual and I disconnect and return solid in my own energy.

Similarly, you can use different variations of this. You could point your foot towards the window or rubbish bin or you can place one or both hands out of view with your fingers pointing towards the earth with the intention their energy will disperse into the ground. Alternatively, you could just visualise the energy dispersing. One man I was talking to explained how when he was a child his mum would constantly tell him off. His father was always reassuring him *"Take no notice, let it go - like water off a duck's back."* Since then, whenever he is in company that he finds challenging or draining, he literally pictures a duck with water running off its back. If you do decide to add any of these tools to your tool belt, make sure to be discrete so the other person does not realise what you are doing!

This technique can also be used when visiting anyone who is very critical of us, or if there is someone with whom we work who frequently puts us or others down. We don't have to let their vibration in. We don't have to let their comments hurt or upset us. Their rant has nothing to do with us. It is a reflection of where they are at themselves. We have nothing to gain by letting this into our hearts or affect our vibration. If you can rise above it and be the better person who goes through your steps and asks for Divine/angelic assistance for the other person, then that's wonderful.

However, if you are in self-preservation mode you can simply position your foot towards the door or point your finger(s) to the floor with the intention that their rant stays outside of you and picture it disperses outside. If we let it in, it will hurt and bring us down. We will lose part of our own enthusiasm or confidence and may respond in a manner that we later regret.

Before coming into their company, or as we see their names come up on our phone, we can go through our steps. We already know they are not in a good emotional space; we know there is nothing to gain by feeling their anger, frustration or jealousy. We can ensure we remain disconnected and strong in our own energy before the conversation takes place. By putting this into practice it will be less difficult to be in their company.

When the conversation starts, we intentionally have our foot pointing towards the door, having made a conscious decision that we will not feel their negativity. We are deciding not to participate the way we have done previously. By stepping off the merry-go-round of the past, whereby they say X then we say Y then they say XX and we say YY the conversation has to now go in a different direction. It may even surprise us and become a pleasant exchange.

*****

Sometimes it is the opposite problem. The energy we are picking up on is our nearest and dearest that is in emotional or physical distress. Because of our closeness to this person, we struggle with disconnecting. We want to help; we really want them to be okay.

I use an analogy to explain this. Consider that your new mother-in-law has just phoned to say she is calling for lunch. You have run out of bread and you know your friend Kate is going into the shops that morning. You phone her and ask her to pick up some bread for you. Kate has been to your home many times and knows what type of bread you like to eat. You chat for a few minutes then hang up.

Five minutes later you phone her back and ask which store she is getting the bread in. You suggest she gets it in the corner store, changing your mind you then suggest she would have more choice in the larger store, or if she went to the bakery, it would be fresher, but then it would be more expensive. Another five minutes pass and you phone her again, where did she park, if it starts to rain will the bread get wet? Has she got a waterproof shopping bag with her? If she is getting other groceries will your bread get squashed? Kate has been your lifelong friend, she knows you inside out, and yet you don't trust her to help you out with your simple request.

When we are asking for Divine intervention on behalf of our loved ones, we need to follow our steps. Having asked for assistance, we need to disconnect and return to our own energy. We need to trust God to get the bread. It may not always be the loaf we would have picked but this *friend* also knows us (and those we pray for) inside out and can see the bigger picture. We need to hand it over.

There is a bible quote that really gives me comfort and reassurance when I am faced with adversity.

"Therefore, I tell you, whatever you ask in prayer,

believe that you have received it,

and it will be yours."

Mark 11:24

Helping Trapped Souls

If you are someone who assists trapped souls you will need to add some extra codes. The first thing to know is that just because you have this ability it does not mean you have to use it. You can ask to be released from this work. If you do decide to assist souls, you really need to set very clear rules by which you are prepared to do this work. I compare this to writing a detailed job description.

JOB DESCRIPTION

NAME:

Terms of employment:

I am prepared to work with souls on the following conditions:

- I am always protected.

- I work with souls that are in the light.

- I work with souls that wish to transition to the light.

- If a soul is not yet ready to transition, they must step back from my energy and my space until such time as they are ready to do so.

- Any of this work I do is for the greater good.

Knowing that my rules are set clearly, I let go my fears around my work and know that I am always held safe. I have got used to the fact that I can be asked for assistance even when I think I am on time off. This was the case when I called to visit a friend for tea. She has graciously taken the time to share her story.

A MOTHER'S LOVE

ALLI-MAI

A number of years ago I was drawn to an old seventeenth century house close to where I live. It's nestled between the foot of a hill and a lake with a river running close by. It's a sort of a lodge house and while it is unlived in it's not derelict, yet in need of a lot of repair. It has high chimneys and sits at the end of a short sweeping driveway lined with really big trees. Some of these trees are in danger of toppling due to their age and the new regularity of stronger storms that we've been having.

My intrigue with the house led me to innocently trespass one day as I was keen to see in and around the place. When walking around the house I couldn't help but feel a mixed sense of something. On one hand there was a strangeness, a sort of restlessness and on the other a sense of a happy jolly sort of place like it may have been back when it was originally built. I particularly sensed this towards the front of the house around a piece of ground that I found out later used to be the garden. Now it's just a jumble of meadow grasses, wildflowers and encroaching briars and blackthorn. After that visit and on some inquiry, I had heard that the place had a sad history attached. A young woman had apparently thrown herself into the lake. The place was supposedly haunted, although I didn't hear of any actual stories of haunting events.

In the weeks that followed I found myself walking that way a lot and several times was drawn to walking in around the house again but only briefly. Also, at that time I found my general demeanor and mood had dipped quite considerably. I felt more and more down but didn't have any particular reason to be that way at that time. Then Bríd visited me one evening for tea and a chat. When she came into the house, she immediately felt very cold. Funny that, I told her, as recently I myself had found it the same, even though the heating had been on and was generally working fine. Bríd sensed a presence in the house and immediately described that it was female. She asked me where I had been recently and who I was around, and that's when I told her about the house. She felt straight away that this woman in spirit had literally followed me home from that house. Bríd could describe the house without me having told her.

I wasn't freaked out or scared as I had known Bríd a while and I am very open to this type of thing. Bríd explained that she felt that the woman was drawn to my energy, it being safe, friendly, warm and had hoped that perhaps she would find help by tagging along with me. Bríd also asked if I had been feeling down of late as she was picking up that this was the energy of the woman. It all made sense. Bríd knew the woman needed to be crossed over to the light as she seemed to be stuck here. Bríd asked that we both close our eyes and pray for the woman, and so Bríd started to say a crossing-over prayer for the woman, and it was then that her story appeared to unfold to us.

As Bríd began to talk we both had an image of two men holding a woman, she had her hands tied behind her back. There was a third man who was in charge and instructing the other two men, he was related to the woman in some way. As the two men pulled her away, they were heading towards the lake shore, the woman bent way over crying and struggling, she knew what was coming. It was then we realized she was pregnant and in her desperation was trying to protect her unborn child.

I wasn't shown anymore but I knew she was purposely drowned because it seemed she was pregnant out of wedlock and by someone not approved of by her family, which is something that would have happened back in those days. As Bríd repeated the prayer several times the energy began to feel different, in fact it changed profoundly, it became lighter, freer, and warmer.

We both saw an image of her holding the hand of a small child, a boy, she seemed serene. They were gone into the light and now free from the injustice and the terrible painful ending she endured during her lifetime. I felt the whole experience was incredible. Her soul, the spirit of that woman, could not let go until her story was told and the truth of what happened was revealed and said aloud, and that she could be shown and helped to go to the light to God. I was privileged to have been part of it. Because of Bríd's knowledge and understanding of the needs of those who have passed, her truly Divine and blessed gift, her true-hearted intention to help all others, including those who have passed, it was all possible. It was truly incredible and left us with a deep sense of gratitude and connection to a higher energy. It also meant my mood got back to normal and my house became warmer again.

Customs, traditions and invocations

Many of our customs in Ireland have been passed down from Pagan times and adjusted to fit in with Christian beliefs. Some of these are to do with protection. One, which thankfully is no longer practiced, used to occur annually on the Feast of St. Martin. A cockerel would be sacrificed and its blood sprinkled on the four corners of the house. Many other invocations also focus on the four corners. Some invoke the energy of earth, fire, wind and water. There is a shamanic invocation that invokes the energy of the Great Serpent of the south, Mother Jaguar to the west, the Hummingbird of the North and Great Eagle of the East to create a sacred space. Personally, I ask Archangel Michael for protection. The prayer I use is of a similar theme.

"Archangel Michael, to my north, to my south, to my east, to my west, above and below,

protecting me and mine now and always.

Thank you."

Another very old Irish custom is *The Ever-living Fire,* believed to have special properties including protection. It is associated with St. Brigid who learned this custom from her father's people, though it was pagan in tradition. She kept a fire available to the poor and the traveller. The fire was kept alight by women, who took turns at night looking after the flame. Some keep a flame alight today in her memory, to ask her protection.

The Hebrides had a very old tradition of blessing their family and property in which they used a handwoven rope called a Súgán Girdle. The rope would be placed in the shape of a circle approximately two meters in diameter in the centre of the floor. The Celts believed in the enchanted circle. When they went through the circle, or stood in it, they believed they were encircled by God's presence and care. Members of the household would take their turn to stand in the circle and say the following words:

"The sacred Three

My fortress be.

Encircling me

Come and be around

My heart and my home."

An old prayer associated with St. Colmcille also incorporates the circle of protection. Many more recent rituals and customs follow the same theme.

"Bless to me the sky that is above me.

Bless to me the ground that is beneath me.

Bless to me the friends who are around me,

Bless to me the love of the Three,

Deep within me and encircling me."

There are numerous similar invocations like Saint Patrick's Breast Plate or The Canticles of the Creatures by Saint Francis. Using these we are reminding ourselves that we are already protected by a greater power. It was not magic but a reminder, through action, that we are always surrounded by God and held in his protection. We are programming ourselves to live in the knowledge that we are safe. Every morning while walking I will include mantras in my conversation with God that include:

Thank you for always keeping me safe.

Thank you for allowing me to walk in your light.

I am loved, blessed, safe and protected.

I believe it as an absolute fact that I am protected and held safe. Yes, I may still have some scary or unpleasant moments in my life, but I know there is a greater power that holds me in His palm. This does not entitle me to a free pass in life, where I only have good experiences, but comforts and reminds me of a constant Divine presence.

When I do encounter something unpleasant, I no longer need to step into unnecessary fear. I know that I am always protected. Similar to Ruth in the story above, once I have my tools in place, I feel safe to use my psychic codes to open up and feel what is going on around me in a more fulfilling way. Whatever you decide to do (bloodletting aside!) to protect you and yours, chose something that you personally connect with.

The following is another lovely old prayer of invocation, it's called *'Caim'*.

"The Holy Three protecting be

Enfolding me in eternity

To shield, to save

To circle, to surround

238

My house, my home

My work, my play

Each night, each day

Each dark, each bright

In Your light

Forever may it be

Now and in eternity."

SELF ACCEPTANCE

By living my life to the full I endeavour to embrace all of my DNA. I am not defined by just one strand. The more grounded I have become, the more I am able to embrace my empathic ability. This may sound like a paradox. But I am now able to understand it. I frequently, if not on a daily basis, pick up on the energy of others who are in difficulty. I follow my steps and return solid to who I am. My life is now more complete than ever before.

For so much of my life I went around like a giant sponge soaking up copies of the energy of those in emotional turmoil and holding onto it, thinking it was mine.

The following testimonial definitely made me smile as I too can recall many moments when I was the reluctant empath.

THE RELUCTANT EMPATH

TERESA

Two of my friends recommended that I make an appointment with Bríd so I went along not knowing what to expect other than my friends were very happy with their treatments. What I remember most from my first session was my grandfather in spirit passed messages to me. During the session the CD stopped playing. Bríd asked me who in spirit fixed radios? I remembered that my grandfather used to fix radios, connect aerials, and cables and could even make batteries. In fact, in the 1920's he had the only radio within a twenty-mile radius of his home. I do remember a sense of peace after the session and wanting to go back for more. Over time I went back for further treatments, which changed me and how I lived my life. Throughout these sessions Bríd tuned into how I had felt throughout various episodes in my past and she could identify the events that I had experienced that needed to be resolved and released.

Bríd brought it to my attention that I am empathic, which I immediately dismissed. However, over the course of time and numerous conversations with Bríd I began to realise that what I considered to be normal was in fact an empathic ability. At first, I did not know when I was in other people's energy. I think the first time that it was really brought to my attention was following a visit to an old graveyard that I had never been to before. It was a beautiful day as I drove past this old graveyard. I knew that a relative of my friend was buried in a graveyard in that area but wasn't sure which graveyard it was. I was unsuccessful in locating the grave and after I left, I popped in to see Bríd.

The first thing I noticed when I got to her house was her dog kept barking at me and didn't want to let me in. This was very unusual as the dog had always been very friendly. On entering the house Bríd asked me had I picked up a spirit. I was completely blank and did not understand what that really meant. It transpired that I had picked up a trapped soul from the graveyard. I remember Bríd saying that it was an old lady wearing a long coat. Bríd said some prayers to release this soul to the light. She explained to me that this soul was looking for help to pass on. She had been a good person but because of events in her life had not crossed on.

Early the following summer, my friend, Zoe was working as a cleaner for an Airbnb. The building had originally been an old schoolhouse that dated back to the eighteen-hundreds. It had been renovated and converted into an Airbnb. Zoe phoned me saying that she was very frustrated as she could not manage to defrost the freezer. She had another commitment and had to leave without having time to complete the job before the next guests were due. I said I would do it for her. It took me nearly two hours to complete the task but as Zoe had frequently helped me out in the past, I was happy to help her out. In fact, I was in a really good mental space. I had gone out to the garden and picked daisies and put them in a vase on the kitchen table while waiting for the freezer to finish defrosting.

When I went home my friend Lisa sent me a text. I replied to her question but then added *"It does not matter because I am going to be dead anyway."* Lisa sent me another text as she thought I was messing. I again told her *"I was going to end my life."* I was very calm and relaxed about the fact that I was intending on finishing my life considering that prior to this I had no intention or reason for wanting to die as I was quite content in my life. But in that moment, it was a very matter of fact thing that I was about to do. She rang me immediately and spent the next three hours talking with me. I continued in that matter-of-fact way briefly thinking that I never thought I'd do this, but it was very clear to me that this was what I was going to do.

Poor Lisa was too scared to hang up to drive to my place but eventually the need for me to end my life lifted. Lisa felt it was finally safe to finish the conversation. Very soon after that I was surprised to get a text from Bríd inviting me over for tea. This was a Sunday afternoon about 4pm and very much not the norm for us.

By the time I arrived at her house I had forgotten about the day's events. I was again in great form. Bríd, on the other hand was not, in fact she was very fidgety, seemed very distracted, kept moving from one chair to another and seemed to become more and more narky. She repeatedly asked me if I had brought a spirit with me? Again, I had no idea why she was asking me this as I distinctly remember being in great form. As she became more distressed and agitated, she checked to see if I had a spirit with me.

Bríd described a building that she could see in her mind's eye and asked me if it sounded familiar. It was an exact description of the Airbnb including the neighbouring building. She asked if I had been there. I still did not know what Bríd was getting at. She then identified a young woman who had a very free spirit personality in her short life but because of the restraints of the church at the time was not able to be who she wanted to be – she had died by suicide.

It was then that the penny dropped. I told Bríd how I had been planning my suicide earlier that day. I now understood why Bríd had texted me and invited me over, which was when the suicidal tendency had left me. Bríd had taken on the woman's energy. She then facilitated the woman's soul to pass on to the light, allowing her to finally be the free spirit she was meant to be.

I was completely overwhelmed by the whole experience as the outcome could have been totally different had Lisa and Bríd not sent those text messages. Up to that day I had not believed that I had an empathic ability. I had accepted that a spirit in the graveyard needed help but until I looked back at how close I had come to ending my life I finally realised that this had happened to me. Even after all of this I still hadn't accepted that this was an ability. And I certainly didn't see it as a gift!

That October I had called to Lisa's new workplace to collect a file. On arriving in her office, she was very enthusiastic to show me around. I immediately felt exhausted. By the time I had walked from the door to the couch I had to sit down. It was overwhelming. She went to the kitchen to make me a cup of tea and when she came back in, I was draped over the arm of the couch. I couldn't understand this. It had come on so suddenly and was completely debilitating. I just wanted to get out of there and go home.

On getting into my car, I experienced a terrible pain in my neck. Driving out of the gate I was not able to turn my head to see if there was oncoming traffic. As I drove, I decided that I would take two painkillers as soon as I got home. But as the pain was so unbearable, I decided I would stop at the next petrol station, which would be another ten-minute drive away, to buy some pain killers. I was totally exhausted.

As I was approaching the petrol station the pain was easing so I decided I would wait till I got home. A further ten minutes out the road the pain had left completely and I was able to turn my head again as if nothing had happened. By the time I had reached my house I was back to myself again. Sitting down to a cup of tea I suddenly realised that the person who used to work in that office, before Lisa, had died by hanging, and I had taken on all their symptoms. I had taken on their experience. I immediately rang Bríd and said, *"I think I might be an empath!"*

The following year I found myself running my own Airbnb. I had an apartment that I was renting out. People would book and check in on-line and be given a code to enter the premises which meant I never had to be available to meet and greet. I rarely saw any of my guests except for one young man who rented the apartment for three nights. He sent numerous long text messages before his arrival giving details of the flight, the connection, the bus timetable and he seemed very pleasant. Because of the time the bus arrived at the station, he wasn't able to organise transport the last five miles to the apartment. I found myself offering to collect him, which was completely out of character for me.

On the journey to the apartment, we chatted about his life in the U.K. and his Irish roots and the fact that he also ran an Airbnb in the U.K. The following evening, I bumped into him and he told me of his plans to go sightseeing the next day and asked me for directions. Because he was such a pleasant person, I offered to drive him to a local tourist attraction. Again, this was not at all the norm for me.

On his last day I brought him back to the bus stop for his journey home. He told me he had left me a bottle of wine as a token of his gratitude for my hospitality. I went back to the apartment to clean it for the next guests. The first thing I did was strip the bed and I carried this bundle of laundry in my arms to put in the washing machine. I immediately felt lethargic. I did not have the energy to finish cleaning the apartment which made no sense as ten minutes earlier I was full of beans and looking forward to getting the task completed as I had plans for the afternoon.

I lay on the couch mulling over my loneliness. I felt hopelessness and life seemed pointless. I knew the apartment needed to be cleaned but I couldn't find it in me to do the work. I wanted to phone Zoe to ask her to finish cleaning the apartment, as she had covered for me before when I wasn't available. I was surprised at how exhausted I had suddenly become. I was close to tears because I wasn't able to do a simple job and I wanted my family around me. All of a sudden everything was just too much.

As luck would have it, it was Bríd that I was meeting that afternoon as she needed supplies from my local shop and we had arranged to meet for tea. While I was lying on the couch, she rang to confirm a time to meet. I bemoaned my very sad existence and that I could not be bothered to go out to the coffee shop.

Bríd called straight round to me. As she was walking up the driveway, she immediately identified that I had taken on the energy of the last person to stay in the apartment. She disconnected me from his energy and went and cleared the residual energy from the apartment. I was immediately revived and invigorated and I efficiently finished cleaning the rental property while Bríd went to the shop. On reflection, I recalled the young man telling me how lonely he was and that his life seemed unfulfilled but to me he had seemed quite pleasant in his conversations.

I was finally beginning to realise that I had the empathic ability to take on the energy of others, not just the deceased, but also the living. I went on to discover that I also have the ability to pick up on the physical pain of others. A few weeks later on visiting a friend in the Midlands I felt terrible stomach cramp. I hadn't been ill at all prior to arriving at her house. But the pain I felt left me rocking on the chair. Thankfully, at this stage I had attended one of Bríd workshops for empaths. Having learnt more about my gift I was able to identify that the pain wasn't mine. I was able to discretely ask for Divine assistance for my friend, to disconnect and return to my own energy.

Having let go my own reluctance to accept my gift I now have a much better understanding of this ability. I have the clear head space to enjoy my life. I laugh more, I sing in my kitchen and I feel good. This raises my vibration. By prioritising my self-care, I am of more use as a staff member for my Higher Power.

It is safe to be ourselves, to accept our own life and take on our own labels. The following is a story of a mum who finally accepted it was time to be free from the shackles of other people's opinions.

UNZIP THE CLOUD

ANONYMOUS

A woman? Yes.
A daughter? Yes.
A sister? Yes.
An aunt? Yes.
A wife? Yes.
A mother? Yes.

Yes! I am all of those. So, I'm an expert on all things female? Wrong! On one level I can revel in the fact that I am a keen multi-tasker. However, it comes at a great cost to my mental and physical wellbeing. All too often I walk around under a cloud of *'should haves'* and *'should nots.'* Second guessing what the right thing to do is and in my search for the 'right' answer, speak to my nearest and dearest and actively listen to their opinions, soaking it all in and replaying their instructions in my subconscious.

But doing exactly that, caused mayhem internally for me. Not quite at the level of a breakdown - I like to refer to it as an 'unzipping of my cloud.'

Thanks to a dear friend who took the time to actually hear my silent struggle, I took up her suggestion to meet Bríd. Before I had time to deliberate, I was on route to North Clare.

I was welcomed by beautiful scenery and a wholesome, spiritual person. My time with Bríd allowed me to unzip my cloud. Pouring's of tears, trapped inside of me for nearly six years, trickled. What brought me here, she asked. I didn't really know the answer. Yes, my friend suggested it but I knew deeply that I needed some spiritual unearthing.

What had I kept safely blocked up inside me? Lots! Fear of doing the wrong thing, letting my family down or worse doing the wrong thing for my son with additional needs. The ghostly words etched silently in my mind's eye over the last few years since his diagnosis: *"Don't label him" "No need to tell anyone outside the family" "He might grow out of it"* - translated to me as: Keep it hidden, deal with it yourself and if you're good enough nobody will ever know about it.

Bríd guided me to the sacred place where I took an introspective look at myself and my thoughts. She verbalised what I really needed to hear: *"Your son has done nothing wrong; you and your husband have nothing to hide, you have a wonderful son. He is autistic and he is lucky to have you as his Mum. Tell other people about him. Release it. There's nothing to hide. You can do this."*

Yes! I have nothing to hide. He is beautiful. Both my sons are equally wonderful and wonderous. Freedom at last. Free from the shackles of other people's opinions. Free from self-imposed entrapment.

My journey to Bríd set me on a road I may never have known existed or, worse, may never have dared travel. Self-belief and ridding myself of carrying others' insecurities have helped me unzip my cloud. It is a journey however and I've lots more to travel. To Bríd I owe a huge *Thank You.*

I am very fortunate in that my work frequently brings me into contact with other people with psychic ability. These people have helped me gain a greater understanding of myself. It is wonderful to be able to discuss our unusual challenges and find ways of using it in positive ways. The following story is from one of these very special people. We connected originally because of having a similar ability. She is now an integral part of our healing meditation group. We support and learn from each other.

THE CHILD WHO DIDN'T BELONG
LRM

I'd always felt different as a child. I never felt like I belonged, even though I was very good at 'fitting in' or gelling with other kids. It's like I knew how to blend in. But still I never felt understood. I always sensed things off other children and adults when I walked into a room. I thought it was normal and that everyone was the same. I remember just knowing something was going to happen before it did, or I just had a knowing! I realised over time people didn't like that. I was seen as 'a know it all' so I stopped speaking up for years! I basically blocked it all out. I complied to how I thought I was supposed to be. Then as a young adult lots more *'situations'* happened, to the point I couldn't block it out anymore and had to accept I had something.

One of those times, a lady walked into where I worked. It was as if a dark circle surrounded her, and the heaviness was so strong, I could feel every bit of her anguish. I knew she was in a dark place, so I sat her down and chatted, she was just in for an appointment, but so much more became of that day. She opened up and told me all the hardship and horrible stuff that happened her. That was the norm for me - I could be out on a night out and a random stranger would come up chatting to me, and before too long they would have told me some of their deepest secrets.

Back then I didn't understand. Now I know straight away and choose to listen or politely walk away. It depends on my own energy that day. Anyway, that lady told me about Bríd. She said she had her book. She offered to give it to me to borrow. That was the beginning of really understanding and finally feeling like I fitted in. So really, she helped me also!!

I read the book and decided to make an appointment with Bríd. Basically, from there, I joined our healing meditation group and I finally felt understood, because all those lovely people understand, and feel the same. The highs, the lows, the dreams, the feelings that aren't yours, but you've to figure out when they are not yours but belong to someone else! I'm still learning and I still go through phases, of blocking it out. But it's great knowing they are always there. Especially Bríd, she just knows when you are not right. I'll be forever grateful for Bríd and our healing meditation group. x

Many of us will have spent much of our lives in and out of the energy of others, possibly influenced by geopathic stress, residual energy and maybe even the energy of souls. Being ourselves can be quite a challenge. For large periods of time, we may have felt different to everyone else, and just wanting to be the same as our siblings and friends.

It is always hugely rewarding for me when I hear back from a client who has embraced the information I have shared and has gone on to incorporate it into their daily life.

USING THE STEPS
ANNA

I feel so grateful and fortunate to have been introduced to Bríd via a mutual friend. I had been having a few challenges in my life so, for me, somebody that could help shine a light was a welcome introduction. I have since been fortunate to have met Bríd a number of times.

Prior to client visits, Bríd reflects on why she feels the person needs help and guidance and, of course, she was spot on for me. She was also able to pinpoint some of my specific traits which may not necessarily be helpful to me and give me guidance on what ways to overcome these.

One of the greatest gifts that Bríd shared with me on my own traits was this of me being an empath, which to be honest I had never heard about prior to meeting her. This revelation has since changed my world. I have a long-term medical condition so have had an inner knowing that I need to change and beginning the journey of understanding life as an empath has provided me with positive life skills.

An empath for me is someone who has the ability to understand the emotional state of other people and for me, at times, it meant taking on copies of others' emotional states. This awareness now has changed my life. Some of the tools that Bríd taught me were to look at my energy levels in proportion to my daily activities. If it wasn't in proportion, then to try and identify who owns it, ask for help for the individual if known, and to disconnect and return to my own energy. She also taught me ways of staying grounded to myself, such as pointing my foot to the door and window.

Bríd has such a wonderful gift and in her presence, she is peaceful, calm, has a lovely sense of humour and is also quite practical and down to earth about life. In my meeting with her, she asked for specific healing on my behalf and I know that I have left meeting her feeling lighter. I have since completed one of her workshops on understanding empaths, which was fabulous, as you meet similar like-minded people and gain insight and skills into life as an empath.

I feel so grateful to have met Bríd in my lifetime and forever appreciate all of her healing and guidance to me.

It can be very challenging for fledgling psychics to accept their new label. Being told you are psychic may seem like the absolute last thing you want to hear. Medication for depression or anger management classes or endless supplies of sage may seem easier options, but when we can embrace this truth, we finally get to be ourselves.

You the reader have now travelled with me on my journey to accepting my sensitivity and empathic ability as psychic gifts. Hopefully it will encourage you to do the same. Knowing that you too may have the ability to sense geopathic stress, residual energy, soul energy and/or pick up on the emotional and physical pain of the living should help you to put some more of your jigsaw pieces together. Alternatively, you may now be aware that a friend or family member is an empath and have come to a much better understanding of their challenges.

Now it is time for you to decipher the codes that work for you. Some of your codes may be old ones that have been passed down through the generations. More may be ones you have worked out for yourself and some may be from this book. Knowing that you have tools at your disposal you can face this fabulous world in the sure and certain knowledge that you are never alone.

It is time to embrace your sensitivity and decipher your personal psychic code.

NOTES

NOTES

NOTES

www.ingramcontent.com/pod-product-compliance
Lightning Source LLC
Chambersburg PA
CBHW020151090426
42734CB00008B/786